E<small>R</small>

The Old Evangelization

How to Spread the Faith
Like Jesus Did

Catholic
Answers
Press

Unless otherwise noted, biblical citations are taken from the Revised Standard Version of the Bible (© 1971 by Division of Christian Education of the National Council of the Churches of Christ in the United States of America).

Published by Catholic Answers, Inc.
2020 Gillespie Way
El Cajon, California 92020
1-888-291-8000 orders
619-387-0042 fax
catholic.com

Printed in the United States of America

Cover design by Theodore Schluenderfritz
Interior design by Sherry Russell

978-1-68357-030-1
978-1-68357-031-8 Kindle
978-1-68357-032-5 ePub

To Nathan Schlueter, who cared enough about my soul to drag me into the Catholic Church.

Contents

JOINING THE BATTLE

BEING A TRULY CATHOLIC EVANGELIST

ACKNOWLEDGMENTS

Over the past quarter of a century and more, many people have influenced and encouraged my evangelization efforts. In particular, Ward Ballard helped me understand evangelization better while I was a Protestant in college, and Fr. Rory Conley initiated the door-to-door campaign in my parish years ago that forced me out of my comfort zone. Also, Maria Ortiz has been a great example of a faithful evangelizer in the parish, the home, and in her circle of influence.

I'm grateful to Bishop Frank Dewane and the Diocese of Venice, Florida, for allowing me to be the director of evangelization there for five years, which allowed me to meet and interact with many good souls throughout the diocese.

I want to thank Todd Aglialoro at Catholic Answers for reaching out to me and encouraging me in this project.

Finally, thanks go to my wife, Suzan, who is one of the best door-to-door evangelists I've ever met and who helped me throughout the process of writing this book; and to my seven wonderful—and patient—children: Anna, Lucy, Maria, Peter, Hope, Madeline, and Lydia.

An Evangelizing Man

I was raised in a Methodist home but embraced Evangelical Protestantism while in high school in the 1980s. As a result, I developed a strong desire to do what Protestants call "evangelism" and Catholics call "evangelization." (At least Catholics call it that when they're not afraid to speak its name.) I fell in love with Jesus and wanted others to experience that love, so I tried to share my faith with others. Not that I was very good at it: I most likely came off as clumsy or holier-than-thou; my nickname in high school was "Joe Bible Stud," if that tells you anything. But my intentions were good, even if I was ineffective.

In college I joined Campus Crusade for Christ (now called "Cru"—I guess having "crusade" in a Christian organization's name is anathema on most college campuses today). This organization had a single focus: to bring people to Christ. We were encouraged to go door-to-door in dorms sharing the gospel, and to take Spring Break trips evangelizing the heathen masses. We were given specific training on exactly what to say, and we enacted mock scenarios to practice sharing the gospel. My experience as an evangelist usually consisted of getting myself psyched up to go out, awkwardly and hurriedly telling people about Jesus, and feeling a rush of relief when it was over.

I was also involved in pro-life work in college, and this led to an unexpected situation: I was now on the other side of the evangelization equation. Most of our pro-life group were Catholic, and some of the members—particularly my roommate, Nate—made it their project to convert me to Catholicism. As you can guess from the fact that this book is published by an organization called Catholic Answers, they were successful.

My conversion to Catholicism didn't diminish my desire to evangelize; it simply redirected it. Initially I used some of the same methods I had used as a Protestant but found them wanting. For almost a decade I searched for ways to tell others about my faith, whether at work, in my neighborhood, or in my parish. Most of my efforts would fall under "trial and error," with the emphasis on "error."

Eventually my parish's young associate pastor approached me about starting an evangelization committee, with me in it (actually, he wanted me to lead it, but didn't tell me that initially). I was happy to help, and he proceeded to form a core group that would evangelize at the parish level, which we did with limited success. Like most parish committees, we probably spent as much time meeting and talking about what we *should* do as actually *doing* it.

Then our parish was assigned a new pastor. When I was introduced to him as the head of the evangelization committee, he immediately said, "So, when are we going door-to-door?" I was overjoyed, for here was a pastor as passionate about evangelization as I was. So we organized door-to-door campaigns, visiting thousands of houses in the parish's surrounding neighborhoods. We also started hosting "Ask Any Question" meetings. These were open meetings at our parish at which I answered any question anyone might have about Catholicism (the group chose me to host the meetings rather than a priest, so that people would feel comfortable enough to ask *any* question). We advertised these meetings at Christmas and Easter in order to reach out to fallen-away Catholics, and also invited the people we met in our door-to-door campaigns. These and other activities met with many successes—though some failures too—and I learned a great deal about evangelization during that time.

Eventually I took a job as a director of evangelization at the diocesan level. While in this position I encountered Catholics from all walks of life and worked with many of them to encourage evangelization efforts throughout the diocese. I discovered a number of evangelization programs created by Catholic apostolates and even created some of my own. And again, I had both successes and failures along the way. I met hundreds of Catholics who wanted to evangelize relatives and friends. Frequently, after a talk I gave or an event I organized, someone approached me to tell the story of a loved one—most often a son or daughter—who was raised Catholic but had left the practice of the Faith. Their pain and sorrow was unmistakable. So was their frustration: many urgently desired to share their faith with those closest to them, but didn't know where to start.

How Would Jesus Evangelize?

For more than a quarter of a century I've been involved in evangelization in some form or another. I've witnessed many different techniques for sharing the Faith and tried many apostolates' evangelization methods. I've heard (and given) countless talks on how we should evangelize. But I've almost never heard anyone talk about how *Jesus* evangelized. As Christians, we look to Jesus as our model in all things. So we should make him our model for evangelization as well.

What I've found is that most Catholics model their evangelization (if they do it at all) on one of two examples: successful corporate marketing or Protestant megachurches. Instead of looking to Jesus, we take Steve Jobs and Joel Osteen as our models. The resulting approaches tend to downplay Catholic doctrine, the Mass, and the "hard" teachings of the Faith, and they aim less at attracting disciples than at gaining cultural acceptance. Ignored is the Church's rich patrimony of evangelizing models and methods, reaching back to Jesus himself.

You've probably heard the term "New Evangelization," which was coined by Pope St. John Paul II. He had good reasons for the term, of course. He understood that we live in a time when there are millions of people who are baptized but not believers. Unlike in previous centuries, when missionaries would travel to foreign lands to evangelize pagans, today's "missionaries" are more likely to focus on fallen-away Catholic neighbors or relatives. In this sense, the kind of evangelization typically called for today is indeed "new."

But I think the term "New Evangelization" is in one way an unfortunate one, because it can be, and often has been, taken to mean a rejection of the "old" evangelization—the two millennia of Catholic missionary efforts by the likes of St. Paul, St. Augustine of Canterbury, St. Francis Xavier, and our Lord himself. As Catholic evangelists we are standing on the shoulders of giants; we should not forget the methods they used to spread the Faith to the farthest reaches of the world. Our situation may be new in some ways, but the essentials of evangelization always remain the same.

A Practical Guide

Each chapter of this book is centered on an encounter Jesus had with someone during his earthly life (and, in one instance, his heavenly life). These are instructive because evangelization is ultimately about personal encounters and one-on-one relationships, not big splashy programs or heavily marketed events. When we see how Jesus interacted with those around him, we witness the perfect evangelizer.

We will also look to the saints to see how they evangelized and learn from their examples. And throughout, I will share my experiences of what has worked and what hasn't worked for me. (Note: all names used in the anecdotes in this book are pseudonyms—except Nate, whom I mentioned earlier. Parish names have also been changed.)

This book isn't intended to help you start a new evangelization program in your parish or diocese. It's intended to be a practical guide for everyday use in your interactions with family, friends, coworkers, and fellow parishioners. We all have a circle of influence, whether we recognize it or not. How we use that influence is up to us. God willing, this book will help you use yours to bring others closer to Jesus Christ in the Catholic Church.

Getting Started

1

Jesus Commands His Disciples to Evangelize

If you're reading this book, you're interested in evangelization. Perhaps you know that Christ commanded it, but you have no idea how to do it. Perhaps the thought of it makes you nervous, or even downright terrified. I'm here to remind you that evangelizing is an essential task for Catholics, and our Lord never gives us a task we can't perform. You don't need a degree in theology, and you don't need to be an eloquent speaker. You just need to have a love for Christ and a desire to tell others about him.

Encounter

The appearance to Mary Magdalene (John 20:1–18)

¹Now on the first day of the week Mary Magdalene came to the tomb early, while it was still dark, and saw that the stone had been taken away from the tomb. ²So she ran, and went to Simon Peter and the other disciple, the one whom Jesus loved, and said to them, "They have taken the Lord out of the tomb, and we do not know where they have laid him." ³Peter then came out with the other disciple, and they went toward the tomb. ⁴They both ran, but the other disciple outran Peter and reached the tomb first; ⁵and stooping to look

in, he saw the linen cloths lying there, but he did not go in. [6]Then Simon Peter came, following him, and went into the tomb; he saw the linen cloths lying, [7]and the napkin, which had been on his head, not lying with the linen cloths but rolled up in a place by itself. [8]Then the other disciple, who reached the tomb first, also went in, and he saw and believed; [9]for as yet they did not know the scripture, that he must rise from the dead. [10]Then the disciples went back to their homes.

[11]But Mary stood weeping outside the tomb, and as she wept she stooped to look into the tomb; [12]and she saw two angels in white, sitting where the body of Jesus had lain, one at the head and one at the feet. [13]They said to her, "Woman, why are you weeping?" She said to them, "Because they have taken away my Lord, and I do not know where they have laid him." [14]Saying this, she turned round and saw Jesus standing, but she did not know that it was Jesus. [15]Jesus said to her, "Woman, why are you weeping? Whom do you seek?" Supposing him to be the gardener, she said to him, "Sir, if you have carried him away, tell me where you have laid him, and I will take him away." [16]Jesus said to her, "Mary." She turned and said to him in Hebrew, "Rabboni!" (which means Teacher). [17]Jesus said to her, "Do not hold me, for I have not yet ascended to the Father; but go to my brethren and say to them, I am ascending to my Father and your Father, to my God and your God." [18]Mary Magdalene went and said to the disciples, "I have seen the Lord"; and she told them that he had said these things to her.

Taking a Step of Faith

In the back row of the crowded meeting room, Claire felt

her blood pressure rising. As an office manager for a family-practice group, she'd found most of the speakers at this medical conference—the first she'd ever attended—helpful and informative. But now a physician's assistant was giving a presentation and talking about abortion in glowing terms.

Claire knew that much of the PA's praise of abortion was unfounded and misleading, but she couldn't bring herself to challenge the speaker in front of hundreds of doctors and nurses during Q&A. With no formal medical training, Claire was a little intimidated by credentialed professionals. Sure, she could teach them a thing or two about maintaining a database, but she'd never considered challenging them on anything marginally medical.

Five years earlier Claire might not have been fazed by a positive mention of abortion. Although she'd grown up Catholic, it was only within the last few years that she'd begun to take her faith seriously. Prayer, Mass, confession, and study of the Church's teachings were now a regular part of her life.

When the talk concluded, Claire was relieved that the training day was at an end and she'd be hitting the road again with her coworkers. Since the conference was held about two hours away from their office, Claire had carpooled with several of the practice's nurses.

As the women discussed the day's presentation, the talk turned to abortion. Two nurses chatted with each other about it positively, calling it a "necessary evil" and describing it as a private choice that is often the best option in a given situation. Though initially quiet, Claire finally felt compelled to say something. After a quick, silent prayer to the Blessed Mother, she remarked, "You know, I don't believe in abortion. As a Catholic I think it's wrong, and . . . well . . . there are better options for women than killing their babies."

You could have heard a suture drop.

Claire feared what would happen next. Would her co-workers ostracize her? Judge her as being, well, judgmental? Might she end up losing her job? Nevertheless, she knew she'd been right to speak up. Soon enough the awkward silence ended and the subject was changed. No one mentioned abortion for the rest of the drive.

When the carpool arrived at the practice's parking lot, everyone said goodbye and hurried to their respective vehicles. But just as Claire was digging her keys out of her purse, one of the nurses, Linda, approached her. "Did you really mean what you said in the car about abortion?"

"Yes. I'm sorry if I offended you, but that's what I believe."

"Okay. Um, I haven't told many people this . . . but eighteen years ago I had an abortion."

Claire didn't know how to respond, so she said nothing. Linda continued with tears in her eyes, "I grew up Catholic, but I quit going to church a long time ago. . . . They say God forgives, but . . . he can't forgive me for what I did. I know he can't."

Claire embraced Linda and said, "Don't ever think that! God can forgive anything. He loves you!" Linda shook her head, unbelieving. Claire went on, "So many women who have had abortions have found healing and peace in the Church."

"Not me. . . . No. I can't believe God can forgive me."

"Linda, I can't imagine the pain you've had to live with. I'm so sorry for you. But you know, there's this special program in the Church, Project Rachel. It's for women who have had abortions. They help you find healing and get right with God and the Church. I can get you connected with them. Would you like me to?"

Linda nodded. "Okay. Maybe . . . maybe I'm finally ready."

Although Claire wasn't well versed in the teachings of

the Church—she probably couldn't explain all the reasons *why* the Church opposes abortion—she was willing to put herself in the crosshairs for her faith. And by doing so, she was able to bring someone closer to Christ. When the Lord called her to be a witness to the value of all human life, she responded in the best way she knew how. Claire told me that she never imagined she would speak up against something her coworkers believed, especially an issue related to medicine. In some ways, she was like Mary Magdalene: a person with little standing in her social circle. But Claire didn't have to be a doctor or theologian—she just had to respond to the Lord's call, as Mary Magdalene did when Christ commanded her to tell others about him.

Mary Magdalene—the Apostle to the Apostles

On that first Holy Saturday, Mary Magdalene was still in shock. Jesus of Nazareth, who had rescued her from demonic possession, and whom she believed to be the long-awaited Messiah, was dead. Not just dead, but disgraced, having been crucified as a common criminal. And now his body lay in the tomb. What about all his promises? What about the coming kingdom he'd preached about? Could it be that he was yet another in a long line of pretenders? No, Mary refused to believe that. Somehow—somehow!—Jesus would still make everything right.

All this may be going through Mary's head as she approaches Jesus' tomb. Drawing closer, she notices something is wrong: the stone has been rolled away. Her heart beats faster, and she rushes to see what's happened. She peers cautiously into the tomb—the Lord's body is gone! Her first thought is that she must tell the apostles—they will know what this means, and what to do.

So she runs off, finds Peter and John, and tells them what she has seen. They come and examine the tomb, but after they depart, Mary stays. She's not sure why, but she knows she wants to stay near to where the Lord's body had lain the day before. Now she can weep, letting her sorrow pour forth. But then she sees . . . *them*: two figures all in white—bright, brilliant white—standing next to the tomb. They ask her, "Why are you weeping?"

She answers, "Because they have taken away my Lord, and I do not know where they have laid him." Then another figure approaches, this one strangely familiar, and yet somehow not.

He too asks, "Why are you weeping?"

Growing anxious, Mary responds, "Sir, if you have carried him away, tell me where you have laid him, and I will take him away."

The strange figure responds simply, "Mary"—and Mary *knows*. She approaches to embrace him, but Jesus tells her, "Do not hold me, for I have not yet ascended to the Father; but go to my brethren and say to them, I am ascending to my Father and your Father, to my God and your God." Christ's first post-resurrection command is for Mary to be a witness to the good news of his resurrection. Jesus wants Mary to *evangelize*.

Christ's resurrection is the greatest miracle in human history, and the climax of salvation history. As St. Paul writes, "If Christ has not been raised, then our preaching is in vain and your faith is in vain" (1 Cor. 15:14). But does Christ choose a king or a religious leader or another important personage to be his first witness? No, he chooses Mary Magdalene, a woman from whom he had cast out seven demons (Luke 8:2). Just as humble shepherds were the first to tell others about Jesus' birth in Bethlehem, so too was the first witness of his resurrection of humble estate.

Mary, then, was an unlikely evangelist. After all, in her world women were not even allowed to be legal witnesses in a trial, so why would anyone trust her as a witness to this far more important event? Yet that is exactly what Christ called her to be. In doing so, he made Mary Magdalene the "Apostle to the Apostles," who preached the gospel (the "good news") to those who would themselves be charged with preaching it to the whole world.

All Are Called to Evangelize

Claire was like Mary Magdalene: someone insignificant in the eyes of the world, with nothing particular in her background to suggest she would be an effective evangelist. Yet when Christ called her, she, like Mary Magdalene, witnessed to what she knew to be true. And in doing so, she brought someone to Christ. Each of us is called to be in some way like Mary Magdalene as well.

"Evangelization" is one of the most popular buzzwords in Catholic circles today: "Be part of the New Evangelization!" "This program will help evangelize fallen-away Catholics!" "Our parish should be an evangelization parish!" Yet the average Catholic is too terrified to actually evangelize. Why? A fear of *rejection*. In our culture, two topics are considered impolite for discussion: politics and religion. To most people, an evangelist is the annoying Jehovah's Witness or Mormon at the door, or the even more annoying neighbor who repeatedly asks you, "Have you been saved?" No one wants to be evangelized while trimming the hedges. And even a faithful Catholic might be afraid that if he evangelizes his friends and family he'll look as if he's shoving his beliefs down their throats.

Yet Christ wants his followers to share their faith—he *commands* them to evangelize. Which presents modern Catholics with a problem: how to obey Christ's explicit command to evangelize without actually, well, evangelizing. To get around this, many of our parishes and "experts" tell us to evangelize "through our actions." In any Catholic discussion of evangelization, you will inevitably hear the quote falsely attributed to St. Francis of Assisi: "Preach the gospel always, and if necessary, use words." (I even have a T-shirt with this quote emblazoned on it.) Besides the fact that there is no evidence that St. Francis ever said this (it wasn't attributed to him until the late nineteenth century), this quote often serves as a dodge. Although people get annoyed with someone who keeps bringing up Jesus at the water cooler or on his Facebook wall, no one complains about a person who is nice and charitable. Fear of being countercultural has led to an overemphasis in evangelization on actions as opposed to words. Yet St. Paul tells us that preaching—sharing the gospel with words—is essential to bringing people to salvation:

> For, "every one who calls upon the name of the Lord will be saved." But how are men to call upon him in whom they have not believed? And how are they to believe in him of whom they have never heard? And how are they to hear without a preacher? And how can men preach unless they are sent? As it is written, "How beautiful are the feet of those who preach good news!" But they have not all obeyed the gospel; for Isaiah says, "Lord, who has believed what he has heard from us?" So faith comes from what is heard, and what is heard comes by the preaching of Christ (Rom. 10:13–17).

The Four "Ps" of Evangelization

The false dichotomy between actions and words is only one of the problems with our understanding of evangelization.

We've also forgotten what evangelization consists of. There are four aspects of sharing one's faith with others, each one vitally important. If a Catholic is going to evangelize, he must integrate all of these aspects, which we can sum up as the four "Ps" of evangelization: Practicing the Faith, Prayer, Penance, and Preaching.

Practicing the Faith

There is truth, of course, in that apocryphal St. Francis quote. A cranky, miserable curmudgeon who tells you of the joy that comes from following Jesus isn't exactly the ideal evangelist. Neither is the person who rejects certain Church teachings but wants you to believe other Church teachings. Personal witness is often the means by which one gains a platform to preach the gospel. People are much more likely to listen to the neighbor who is always ready to help, who is cheerful, and who lives an ordered life than the one who is a moody, selfish slob. They are also more likely to listen to someone who is consistent in his faith rather than to "cafeteria Catholics," who pick and choose what they want to believe and are therefore just witnesses to their own human wisdom, not the wisdom of the Church. In order to be a good evangelist, we have to, as the saying goes, "walk the walk before we talk the talk."

Prayer

I know, I know: of course we have to pray! But before you gloss over this paragraph because it started with a cliché, consider that prayer is essential for successful evangelization for a number of reasons, such as: (1) it allows us to know the will of God more clearly; (2) it makes us more attuned to the promptings of God in specific situations; and (3) it increases charity toward those around us, motivating us to share the gospel with them. Without prayer, evangelizing is futile; it becomes a sterile exercise in sales and marketing. What's the difference between promoting Christ without prayer and promoting Coca-Cola? About ten teaspoons of sugar and some carbonated water. Prayer supercharges our evangelization efforts and makes them God's efforts as well. Prayer, in fact, is so important that we'll devote the next chapter to it.

Penance

Wait, what? What does penance have to do with evangelization? Penitential suffering is an essential ingredient of the whole of Christian life, and that includes evangelization. If you read the letters of St. Paul (the greatest evangelist in Church history), you will see that he often refers to the importance and value of suffering:

> For it has been granted to you that for the sake of Christ you should not only believe in him but also suffer for his sake (Phil. 1:29).

> For his sake I have suffered the loss of all things, and count them as refuse, in order that I may gain Christ and be found in him, not having a righteousness of my own, based on law, but that which is through faith in Christ, the righteousness from God that depends on faith; that I may know him and the power of his resurrection, and may share his sufferings, becoming like him in his death, that if possible I may attain the resurrection from the dead (Phil. 3:8–11).

> Three times I besought the Lord about this, that it should leave me; but he said to me, "My grace is sufficient for

you, for my power is made perfect in weakness." I will all the more gladly boast of my weaknesses, that the power of Christ may rest upon me. For the sake of Christ, then, I am content with weaknesses, insults, hardships, persecutions, and calamities; for when I am weak, then I am strong (2 Cor. 12:8–10).

We are afflicted in every way, but not crushed; perplexed, but not driven to despair; persecuted, but not forsaken; struck down, but not destroyed; always carrying in the body the death of Jesus, so that the life of Jesus may also be manifested in our bodies. For while we live we are always being given up to death for Jesus' sake, so that the life of Jesus may be manifested in our mortal flesh (2 Cor. 4:8–11).

At one point Paul even goes so far as to say, "Now I rejoice in my sufferings for your sake, and in my flesh I complete what is lacking in Christ's afflictions for the sake of his body, that is, the church" (Col. 1:24). This mysterious passage (what could be "lacking" in Christ's afflictions?) points to a reality that Paul understands well: his sufferings, voluntary or not, unite him to Christ and Christ's redemptive work. Paul offers up those sufferings for the salvation of souls.

We can do the same today. We can offer up our involuntary sufferings—perhaps an illness, or a vexing personal situation, or the death of a loved one—for someone else. We are called to embrace voluntary sufferings for others as well—fasting, taking cold showers, refraining from some harmless indulgence. Like prayer, penance offered for others can supercharge our evangelization efforts, and, in some mysterious fashion, both our prayers and our penances can bring people to Christ. As Pope Pius XII wrote:

This is a deep mystery, and an inexhaustible subject of meditation, that the salvation of many depends on the prayers *and voluntary penances* which the members of the Mystical Body of Jesus Christ offer for this intention (*Mystici Corpus Christi* 44, emphasis added).

Preaching

Finally, an essential aspect of evangelization is actually preaching the gospel. With words. Nonverbal communication can say many things, but words can say more, and more effectively. How would Linda have known what Claire believed about abortion if Claire had not spoken up? So, using words is absolutely necessary for evangelization. *What* words to use, and *when* to use them is, however, something that is known through prayer and experience.

Say, for example, that you haven't mentioned your faith to any of your coworkers yet, and that there is one particular person you want to share the gospel with. If you are praying and doing penance for that person, God will likely provide you with an opportunity to evangelize him, and grant you the words as well. Many years ago I had a close coworker who was an atheist. I hadn't told him anything about my faith, but he knew I was a practicing Catholic from a number of things (the ashes on my forehead on Ash Wednesday was probably the biggest clue). One day right before 5:00 p.m. (I was almost out the door!), he entered my office and closed the door. Over the next two hours, he peppered me with questions about God, the cosmos, and the meaning of life. He knew I took these questions seriously, and he wanted to hear what my answers (really, the Church's) were. Of course, such overt opportunities to talk about our faith don't always come up—more often than not we have to be the ones to broach the topic, as Claire did during her carpool. But if we are praying and doing penance, God will sometimes drop opportunities in our lap.

Evangelization is a requirement of being a disciple of Jesus Christ, as can be seen in the actions of the first Christians. The Gospels tell us how Mary Magdalene immediately shared the good news of the resurrection with others, and the Acts of the Apostles is by and large a history of early Christian evangelization.

Of course, if you have read this far, you probably already acknowledge the importance of evangelization. Now, like Mary Magdalene and Claire, you need to get off the couch and do it! I hope the following chapters will give you insights into how you can bring others to Christ in the Catholic Church. Christ is calling you—just as he did Mary Magdalene and Claire—to witness to him in your everyday life. Will you respond?

Example

St. Philip Neri

When we think of evangelists, we usually think of those who travel great distances to bring people to Christ. St. Paul and St. Francis Xavier are the prototypes, and both traveled many miles to spread the gospel. However, more often God calls us to evangelize where we live, and this was the case with St. Philip Neri.

Philip was born in Florence in 1515, but he moved to Rome at the age of eighteen and made it his home for the rest of his life. Philip had a great desire to evangelize, and he hoped to imitate his contemporary St. Francis Xavier in becoming a foreign missionary. He prayed fervently for this and resolved to make it happen.

But before he took further steps he visited a monk in Rome named Augustine Ghettini, who was known for his sanctity. Philip told Augustine of his great desire to be a missionary and asked if it was God's will. Augustine told him to come back in a few days for the answer.

Philip waited anxiously for three days, convinced that foreign missionary work was his calling, and then returned to the monastery—where Augustine told him that St. John the Evangelist had appeared to him and told him that "Philip's Indies were to be in Rome, and that God wished to make use of him there."

Philip accepted this as the Lord's will and spent over sixty years in Rome working tirelessly to help the poor, care for the sick, and evangelize souls. He heard confessions every day, often in great numbers. As St. John had predicted in the monk's vision, the Lord used Philip to bring about the salvation of many souls. Indeed, he became known as the "Apostle of Rome."

Examination

- Am I scared to evangelize? Why?

- Do I understand that evangelization is a lifelong—and everyday—duty for every Catholic?

Exploration

- Why do you think Catholics are afraid of evangelization?

- What is the biggest barrier to evangelization?

- Who is the best Catholic evangelist you know?

Exercise

- Decide on a penance you can perform, such as giving up coffee, taking cold showers, or abstaining from meat. Begin that penance and offer it up for a specific person you wish to evangelize.

- Resolve to say something this week about the Faith to someone not practicing it.

- Look into the life of your favorite saint and find two or three ways he or she evangelized others.

2

Jesus Teaches the Value of Prayer

Okay, you're convinced you need to evangelize, but you don't know where to start. Evangelization appears to have a lot in common with marketing: we're trying to persuade others to "buy" our "product" (Catholicism). But while there are similarities between the two, the differences are more important. In our attempt to "sell" Catholicism we must not forget that conversion is possible only through the power of the Holy Spirit. We need his help for it to happen. This is where prayer comes in. Without prayer, evangelization is a doomed enterprise.

Encounter

The healing of the boy with a "dumb spirit" (Mark 9:16–29)

[16]And he asked them, "What are you discussing with them?" [17]And one of the crowd answered him, "Teacher, I brought my son to you, for he has a dumb spirit; [18]and wherever it seizes him, it dashes him down; and he foams and grinds his teeth and becomes rigid; and I asked your disciples to cast it out, and they were not able." [19]And he answered them, "O faithless generation, how long am I to be with you? How long am I to bear with you? Bring him to me." [20]And they brought

the boy to him; and when the spirit saw him, immediately it convulsed the boy, and he fell on the ground
and rolled about, foaming at the mouth. [21]And Jesus
asked his father, "How long has he had this?" And he
said, "From childhood. [22]And it has often cast him into
the fire and into the water, to destroy him; but if you
can do anything, have pity on us and help us." [23]And
Jesus said to him, "If you can! All things are possible
to him who believes." [24]Immediately the father of the
child cried out and said, "I believe; help my unbelief!"
[25]And when Jesus saw that a crowd came running together, he rebuked the unclean spirit, saying to it, "You
dumb and deaf spirit, I command you, come out of
him, and never enter him again." [26]And after crying
out and convulsing him terribly, it came out, and the
boy was like a corpse; so that most of them said, "He is
dead." [27]But Jesus took him by the hand and lifted him
up, and he arose. [28]And when he had entered the house,
his disciples asked him privately, "Why could we not
cast it out?" [29]And he said to them, "This kind cannot be driven out by anything but prayer and fasting."

"My Prayers Were Answered"

John was frustrated. "You've got to be kidding me!"

I took a breath and tried to remain calm. "No, I'm serious. The Catholic Church will never permit women to
become priests."

"That's insane—why can't the Church get out of the
Dark Ages?"

I was sitting in a small room at my parish church, conducting
an "Ask Any Question" session. We had advertised it at Christmas Masses a few weeks before, hoping to attract "Christmas

and Easter Catholics" who might have misconceptions about Catholicism. Previous sessions had gone well. But now a man in his fifties was making it clear that he was loaded for bear.

He'd begun innocently enough, asking some benign questions about why the Church had changed certain disciplines over the years, such as allowing meat to be eaten on Fridays and permitting girls to be altar servers. But then the questions became more pointed, and John more aggressive. He was never disrespectful, and sincerely wanted to hear my answers. But he was clearly skeptical of the Church's authority and its divine mandate.

Throughout the session, John's wife, Beth, sat quietly next to him, looking somewhat embarrassed. I found out later that she had always been a practicing Catholic, even though her husband had stopped practicing in his thirties. She had prayed for him throughout their marriage, never losing hope that he would return to the Church of his youth. She was glad he wanted to ask these questions, but she also knew he could be a tough nut to crack. After about an hour and a half, the session wrapped up, and John and Beth left.

This was just the first of three sessions we had that month, in order to make it easy for interested people to attend at a convenient time. The idea was that people would need to attend only one session to get their questions answered. But although John and Beth attended the first session, they appeared at the second one too, at which John had more questions. Then they attended the third session, with still more questions from John. Then, after Easter, our parish held another "Ask Any Question" session—and sure enough, John and Beth were there.

In fact, for the next year John attended *all* of our sessions, with new questions (and sometimes follow-ups) each time. But I noticed that over time his questions changed—they were less belligerent and more sincerely inquisitive. I also noticed him attending Mass, even on days other than Sundays. We built up a friendly relationship, though he was often bemused by my adherence to Catholic beliefs and practices.

Then one day I saw Beth without John. I asked her where he was, and she answered, "John died two weeks ago." I was shocked. Beth explained that John had suffered a massive heart attack and, at just fifty-eight years old, died suddenly; there was no warning. But as I talked to Beth, I discovered something wonderful: John had been meeting with our parish priest in recent months. He had been reconciled to the Church, receiving the sacrament of penance for the first time in decades. Beth, despite her sadness, was grateful that her husband had reconciled with God before his death. "We didn't know it was to be his time, but God knew. My prayers were answered." Not only Beth's prayers: the parish evangelization committee had been praying for John, as had our priests and John's daughter and son-in-law as well. Like the desperate father who brought his son to Jesus for healing, they all had faith that their prayers could make a difference.

Lack of Faith

The image of Jesus in the Gospels is one of a person under control: "I lay down my life, that I may take it again. No one takes it from me, but I lay it down of my own accord. I have power to lay it down, and I have power to take it again; this charge I have received from my Father" (John 10:17–18). No power on earth can overcome him, and no obstacle can hinder him from his mission. Even when he's undergoing his Passion, it's clear that he is only pursuing his own mysterious plan. The same cannot be said, however, of his apostles. In marked contrast with Jesus, they appear at times confused, self-centered, frightened, and powerless.

The story of the boy with the "dumb spirit" is a case in point. When his father approaches Jesus, he has already approached the apostles, and they have failed to heal the boy. Yet the father does not give up; even if Christ's closest disciples can't heal his son, the man believes, perhaps Jesus can do what they are unable to. When he tells Jesus his predicament, there is a note of exasperation in the Lord's response: "O faithless generation, how long am I to be with you? How long am I to bear with you? Bring him to me." Notice his condemnation: "O *faithless* generation." He is not condemning the father, who is showing faith by approaching Jesus after the apostles failed—he is condemning the apostles, who did not have the faith they needed to heal the boy. They didn't trust in God's power to heal him—they didn't really believe it was possible.

Jesus continues to emphasize the role of faith in his exchange with the father. When the desperate man asks Jesus to perform the healing "if you can," Jesus responds—again with a hint of exasperation: "If you can! All things are possible to him who believes." This powerful statement—"All things are possible to him who believes"—can be found on pillowcases and Bible covers everywhere, which may have diminished its strength. Is it really true that *all* things are possible for the one who believes? I can get that job I want? I'll be able to afford to send my kids to college? My son who has been away from the Church for years will return? Perhaps if we're honest with ourselves, we'll see that we don't really believe "all things" are possible. Our own experience of failure and disappointment in life teaches us that some things are just not possible. Yet our Lord challenges us to reject that limited view.

The desperate father sees his faith as a life preserver: "I believe; help my unbelief!" I can't think of a more beautiful statement of faith. It is the humble plea of someone who feels completely powerless. And this is exactly when our Lord answers his plea and heals the boy.

Later, in private, the apostles ask Jesus to explain what happened. Why couldn't they heal the boy? Did they do something wrong? Jesus once again chides their lack of faith: "This kind cannot be driven out by anything but prayer and fasting." In other words, they trusted in their own power, but it is only by depending on God that they have any hope of performing such a miracle.

For some years I did evangelization work in an area with a lot of elderly retirees. As I traveled to various parishes, I heard the same concern over and over: "My son [or daughter or grandson or granddaughter] has left the Church, and I don't know what to do. Do you have any advice?" The pain behind the question was always evident; as a parent, I can think of no greater tragedy than for one's child to abandon the Church. But I also observed a certain desperate hope for a ready-made solution, an easy way to "fix" their child and bring him or her back to the Faith. I would, of course, offer them the kinds of suggestions and advice you'll find in this book. But over and over again, I would encourage them first and foremost to pray. To pray as they'd never prayed before. To pray as St. Monica did for her son St. Augustine. And fast if they could. Ultimately, I told them, it would only be through the power of God that their children would return to the Church. So even if they had no contact with their children, they still possessed a great weapon in the battle for their children's souls: prayer.

Do We Believe?

When we see how hard it is to overcome evil, there are two ways we typically react. At one extreme, we just give up. So if a loved one has left the Church, we give up hope that he will return.

At the other extreme, we dive into the problem, believing that if we just work hard enough, we can fix anything. We can *make* our son or daughter or other loved one return to the Church. We turn them into our "project," constantly badgering them, believing that will eventually bring them into the loving arms of God. I call this the "American syndrome." It's part of the American mythology that if we just roll up our sleeves and have a "can-do" spirit, there's nothing we can't accomplish.

But in both reactions—resignation and overzealous efforts—we fall into the sin of pride, trusting only our own powers rather than God's. Just because our own powers are inadequate to effect a certain change doesn't mean that God can't make it happen. Conversely, even when our efforts are effective we aren't truly in control.

In both cases the missing element is prayer, which acknowledges that God has the power to do what we cannot, and that whatever power we have to accomplish something comes from him. That's why, as I argued in the last chapter, we can't succeed in evangelization without praying.

Then why don't we do more of it? The average Catholic prays only about two to three minutes a day. (Okay, I just made up that stat, but I bet you believed it, didn't you? Sounds reasonable.) Yet we spend many hours watching TV, surfing the Internet, and doing other recreational activities. Our actions speak loudly of our priorities. If we are serious about evangelization, we need to be serious about prayer. Saints and spiritual directors have often recommended at least an hour of prayer a day. That might sound unrealistic for you, and it might not happen overnight—and in fact one should work up to it—but it's a goal we should strive for if we want to succeed in evangelization.

But you may be thinking: I'm too busy; I don't have an extra hour a day! When Fulton Sheen encountered this objection, he responded, "Then you need to pray *two* hours a day!" There is quite literally nothing more important than prayer. We must treat it like the foundation for everything in Catholic life that it is.

Prayer, Practically Speaking

But let's go beyond the generalities—"we need to pray!"—and get specific. Prayer is involved in evangelization in three separate ways:

1. We pray for ourselves—for strength, wisdom, and guidance.

2. We pray for those we are evangelizing.

3. We encourage those who are away from God to pray.

Let's look at each one in turn.

First, we need to pray for ourselves. You know the drill when you get on an airplane. The flight attendants tell you that, in case of an emergency, you should put your own oxygen mask on, then put masks on your kids. I don't know one parent whose instinct wouldn't be "I'm putting my kid's mask on first—he's more important than me!" But, of course, the problem is that before you got the mask on your squirming kid you'd have dropped unconscious. You must first take care of your own oxygen so you're around to take care of your child's. The same is true in the work of evangelization. You can't help anyone draw closer to Christ unless *you* are close to him. So you need to pray for yourself.

Second, we pray for those we're evangelizing. I'll admit, I tend to be a "list prayer" guy. Meaning I pray in lists, "Lord, I pray for Dave, Dawn, Jared, Amy, and Steve." While that's better than nothing, I believe that the Lord wants us to be more specific in our prayers. "I pray for Dave, that he will find some good Catholic friends who can witness your love to him." Why does this matter, if God already knows what would be best for him? First, I think it helps us: praying for specific things makes us meditate on what God wants for us and our loved ones. Second, God delights in answering prayers. If you say, "I pray for Dave," how can you ever know that your prayer has been answered? But by praying for specific things, you can glorify God when those prayers are answered.

Third, we should encourage those we are evangelizing to pray. Although many don't realize it, everyone needs prayer. We live in a desperate world, and people all around us— our neighbors, the parents of the other students at our kids' school, someone in the grocery line with us—are in dire need of God's love, but they don't know that love is as close as a whispered prayer. By encouraging others to pray, we start them on a path back to God and his love.

I witnessed first-hand the power of encouraging others to pray when my pastor and I started a door-to-door evangelization campaign for my parish. Around fifty parishioners went to the neighborhoods in our parish to promote it and tell people about Catholicism. I designed the following basic script for our efforts:

- Introduce yourself.
- Say that you are representing St. Cecilia's.
- Invite them to come to the inquiry meeting that will be held on [date].

- Give them a bag of materials [this included a Rosary, an apologetics booklet, and information about Mass and confession times at the parish].
- Thank them for their time.

Our intention was to be brief and informative. Of course, if someone wanted to ask questions we'd be open to that, but we tried not to ask too much of their time. After our first outing, everyone gathered back at the parish to compare notes. Most of us had similar experiences: we were met with little interest and mostly rushed interactions. But one woman reported a much higher level of interaction with the people she met. She told us that, before leaving the house, she would simply ask, "Is there anything you would like me to pray for with you?" In many cases, this opened the floodgates. First, it showed the person that we weren't there to *get* something, but to *give* something. Everyone is hurting in some way, and everyone has something for which they need prayers. Many of the residents this volunteer visited opened up about things that were troubling them, and she was able to intercede for them. Just as important, *they* often prayed *with* her: her invitation opened up the power of prayer for them to experience directly. Needless to say, I quickly added "Ask for prayer requests" to the basic script.

On a later campaign, when a fellow parishioner and I approached a certain house, the owner—an older woman—was at her mailbox. I told her why we were there, and she listened patiently. Then I asked her if there was anything she'd like us to pray for, and she began to cry. Her husband had died just a few days before, and she felt her loss greatly. So right then and there we stood on her street corner and prayed for her—and with her—for the next ten to fifteen minutes. She was a member of the local Evangelical church, but as I was leaving she told me that she would always think highly of our Catholic parish because of what we had done that day.

Imagine the Possibilities

Never underestimate the power of prayer. Beth prayed for her husband, John, for years—decades, even—and saw no results; she could be forgiven for thinking that her prayers were useless. Yet she continued to pray, and before his death John was reconciled to the Church. Similarly, the father of the boy with the "dumb spirit" was disappointed when the apostles couldn't heal his son. Yet he still went to Jesus in supplication, and his prayers were answered.

No one wins an Olympic race without discipline. No one becomes CEO of a successful company without discipline. Likewise, no one becomes a good evangelizer without discipline. And the first application of discipline is in the life of prayer. If you are not yet committed to prayer, please put this book away until you are. The advice that follows this chapter is useless without prayer, but *with* prayer it can bear abundant fruit. To paraphrase our Lord: "All things are possible to him who *prays*."

Example

St. Thérèse of Lisieux

From a very young age, Thérèse of Lisieux—the "Little Flower"—wanted to be a missionary. Raised in a devout Catholic home, she wrote that at the age of fourteen "I experienced a great desire to work for the conversion of sinners, a desire I hadn't experienced so intensely before." She yearned to travel to foreign lands and convert pagans to Christianity. If all one knows about the rest of her life story is that she became a cloistered nun and died at the age of twenty-four—one might think that her desire wasn't fulfilled. Yet it was, so much so that Pope Pius XI in 1927 named her co-patron of the missions. How is it that the Little Flower was a missionary? Through the power of her prayers.

Around the same time that she felt the call to evangelize, she learned of an unrepentant criminal named Henri Pranzini, who was sentenced to death for the gruesome killing of three women: a socially prominent woman, her daughter, and her servant. Thérèse yearned for this man to be converted before his execution—but how could a fourteen-year-old girl help to bring that about? She writes in her autobiography, *The Story of a Soul*: "I wanted at all costs to keep him from falling into hell, and to succeed I employed all means imaginable, feeling that of myself I could do nothing. I offered to God all the infinite merits of our Lord."

She couldn't talk to Pranzini, but she could talk to the One on whom his eternal destiny rested. She could do nothing, yet she could do everything! So she continued to beseech God for Pranzini's conversion up until the very moment of his execution.

The day after Pranzini's execution, Thérèse read this in the local paper:

[Pranzini] turned, took hold of the crucifix the priest was holding out to him, and kissed the sacred wounds three times! Then his soul went to receive the merciful sentence of him who declares that in heaven there will be more joy over one sinner who does penance than over ninety-nine who have no need of repentance!

Through the prayers of a young girl, a soul was lifted up to heaven.

A young girl who lived only twenty-four years, most of them in a convent, is considered by the Church the model for all missionaries—that is the importance of prayer!

Examination

- Am I committed to praying every day, for myself and for my loved ones?

- Do I pray specifically for my evangelization efforts, that God might use me in the conversion of others?

Exploration

- How does prayer transform evangelization into something more than marketing?

- Why couldn't the disciples cast out the "dumb spirit" from the boy—and what does that mean for us?

- How does our American do-it-yourself culture work against evangelization?

Exercise

- Determine a specific time of day—preferably the early morning—and resolve to pray every day at that time for at least ten minutes longer than you currently pray daily. Increase your time in prayer every month until you are praying for an hour a day.

- Pick one person in your life who needs to become Catholic or to return to the Catholic faith. Pray for that person every day, specifically asking for his or her conversion.

- Study the life of St. Thérèse of Lisieux, and in particular how she evangelized even while living as a cloistered nun.

3

Jesus Does More than Welcome Others

Before we start evangelizing, we should know what our objective is. After all, you can't accomplish anything in life if you haven't identified your goal. What's the objective of evangelization? For many Catholics today, it's to be "welcoming." Every parish wants to be a "welcoming" parish, and every Catholic wants to welcome others to the Catholic faith. But what happens when we make "welcoming" the be-all and end-all of evangelization? We avoid tough topics, or even excuse lifestyles or beliefs incompatible with Catholicism, putting souls in danger.

Encounter

The confrontation with the Pharisees and scribes (Luke 11:37–52)

[37]While he was speaking, a Pharisee asked him to dine with him; so he went in and sat at table. [38]The Pharisee was astonished to see that he did not first wash before dinner. [39]And the Lord said to him, "Now you Pharisees cleanse the outside of the cup and of the dish, but inside you are full of extortion and wickedness. [40]You fools! Did not he who made the outside make the inside also?

[41]But give for alms those things which are within;

and behold, everything is clean for you. [42]But woe to you Pharisees! for you tithe mint and rue and every herb, and neglect justice and the love of God; these you ought to have done, without neglecting the others. [43]Woe to you Pharisees! for you love the best seat in the synagogues and salutations in the market places. [44]Woe to you! for you are like graves which are not seen, and men walk over them without knowing it."

[45]One of the lawyers answered him, "Teacher, in saying this you reproach us also." [46]And he said, "Woe to you lawyers also! for you load men with burdens hard to bear, and you yourselves do not touch the burdens with one of your fingers. [47]Woe to you! for you build the tombs of the prophets whom your fathers killed. [48]So you are witnesses and consent to the deeds of your fathers; for they killed them, and you build their tombs. [49]Therefore also the Wisdom of God said, 'I will send them prophets and apostles, some of whom they will kill and persecute,' [50]that the blood of all the prophets, shed from the foundation of the world, may be required of this generation, [51]from the blood of Abel to the blood of Zechariah, who perished between the altar and the sanctuary. Yes, I tell you, it shall be required of this generation. [52]Woe to you lawyers! for you have taken away the key of knowledge; you did not enter yourselves, and you hindered those who were entering."

All Are Welcome in this Place

One of the most popular hymns in Catholic parishes for the past couple of decades has been "All Are Welcome" by Marty Haugen. The lyrics include:

Let us build a house where love can dwell
and all can safely live,
a place where saints and children tell
how hearts learn to forgive.
Built of hopes and dreams and visions,
rock of faith and vault of grace;
here the love of Christ shall end divisions.
All are welcome, all are welcome,
all are welcome in this place.

To me, "All Are Welcome" sounds more like the theme song for *Cheers* ("Sometimes you want to go where everybody knows your name") than a Catholic hymn. Why then is it so popular as such? Because it expresses what many Catholics feel is the ingredient essential to evangelization: welcome.

I met once with an evangelization committee that wanted ideas for creating a spirit of evangelization in their parish. First I asked the group to tell me what they thought evangelization was, and how practically to go about it. One middle-aged man said, "We really need to be welcoming. I think that's the key. People need to come to St. Ann and know that they are welcome." Others in the group agreed.

I wasn't surprised by the man's answer, for I had heard it many times. The Catholic Church had for years been unwelcoming, I was told, and that's why so many people had left it. If parishes became more welcoming, more non-Catholics would enter the Church and more lapsed Catholics would return to it.

When I asked the committee members what it meant, exactly, to be more welcoming, they mentioned things such as friendly ushers, explicit greetings from the pastor, and welcome statements in the bulletin. I wanted to probe deeper, however, so I continued to push them to define what they meant by a "welcoming" parish. That's when they pointed out how much less welcoming Catholic parishes seem than the typical Protestant church. They had images of friendly faces, exuberant "fellowship," and pews bursting at the seams. They wanted to be more like that, and to banish from the parish anything that might make a person feel unwelcome.

Yet is this really the right approach? Is welcoming the primary means of evangelization? As always, it's helpful to look to the example of Jesus Christ. He wasn't as welcoming as we might imagine.

I Have Come to Bring Division

Most people—including those who have never cracked open the Gospels—have a vague mental image of Jesus Christ. Typically, it is one of gentleness, kindness, and mildness. But that image comes from popular culture, not from the Gospels. Check out a few biblical examples of the "kinder, gentler" Jesus:

Do you think that I have come to give peace on earth? No, I tell you, but rather division; for henceforth in one house there will be five divided, three against two and two against three; they will be divided, father against son and son against father, mother against daughter and daughter against her mother, mother-in-law against her daughter-in-law and daughter-in-law against her mother-in-law (Luke 12:51–53).

And if your hand or your foot causes you to sin, cut it off and throw it from you; it is better for you to enter life maimed or lame than with two hands or two feet to be thrown into the eternal fire (Matt. 18:8).

And if any one will not receive you or listen to your words, shake off the dust from your feet as you leave that house or town (Matt. 10:14).

If a man does not abide in me, he is cast forth as a branch and withers; and the branches are gathered, thrown into the fire and burned (John 15:6).

There are many other such examples, including John 6:53, 14:6, and 15:6; and Matthew 8:21, 5:29, 5:48, and 10:34. Imagine your parish priest speaking as Jesus did: threatening people with eternal fire, saying he wants to divide families, and dismissing those who reject his words. Would anyone call that priest "welcoming"? Of course not. Yet his language would be no different from Jesus'.

We see Christ being especially unwelcoming to the religious leaders of his day—those who were tasked with leading others to God. In chapter 11 of Luke's Gospel, Christ appears exasperated—as if he has finally lost his patience with the Pharisees. When they criticize him for not performing the ritual washings before eating, he launches into a harsh litany of accusations against them, calling them fools, and three times telling them, "Woe to you!" The lawyers who are also hearing this feel unfairly included in Christ's criticisms, being that they practice their faith in a manner similar to that of the Pharisees. "Teacher, in saying this you reproach us also," they say (Luke 11:45).

Imagine a similar exchange today at your local parish. Fr. Larson gives a homily about the heavy toll that divorce takes on children. This should, of course, be non-controversial, as multiple studies have proven, and common sense affirms, that divorce is harmful to children. But Joe left his wife and children years ago, and he's stung by the implication that he shouldn't have. So he approaches Fr. Larson after Mass and tells him he's hurt by Father's words. If Fr. Larson is like most people today, he will be quick to apologize and do all he can to make Joe feel more comfortable. He might even tell Joe that he thinks Joe's situation is an exception; otherwise, Joe might feel unwelcome at the parish and decide to leave for another one, or even leave the Church entirely. In seeming to excuse Joe's sin, then, Fr. Larson ensures that Joe will never confront it and take the necessary steps to be reconciled with God and his family.

But what does Jesus say in response to the lawyers who are complaining, in essence, "You hurt our feelings!" "Woe to you lawyers also!" Jesus thunders, and launches into a harsh denunciation of their ways. Now, when reading this Gospel passage, and others like it, we may simply think, "Pharisees and lawyers = stereotypical bad guys." They are just foils for Christ, and not real people. But they *are* real people, made in the image of God—people Jesus came to die for. Is Christ's harsh condemnation of them somehow inconsistent with his love for them?

The only reason it might appear so to us is that we have a simplistic notion of what it means to love our neighbors. We think of it strictly as being nice to them. Yet we know that Christ loved everyone and yet wasn't "nice" to all of them. In fact, if you read through the Gospels you find that Jesus rarely *ever* appears "nice" as we moderns would define it. On the contrary, he is usually abrupt, sparing with compliments, and willing to confront others directly about their failings. He appears not to follow Dale Carnegie's advice about "how to win friends and influence people." Yet he has a deeper love for every individual than we will ever imagine. How do we square this apparent circle?

What's Our Goal?

To repeat: many well-intentioned Catholics have misidentified the goal of evangelization. They erroneously see it as creating a welcoming community that people will want to join. If we are nice enough, they think, everyone will want to be our friends. But that was not the goal of Jesus Christ. His goal was to convert sinners, to rescue souls from damnation and bring them to their eternal reward in heaven. Once you see how his goal differs from that of most Catholic evangelizers, you will recognize that the methods to achieve those goals will also differ.

Note, however, that Christ's methods were not one-size-fits-all, and neither should ours be. The way he dealt with the Pharisees is much different from his interactions with the Samaritan woman at the well (John 4) or the woman caught in adultery (John 8:1–11). In Ecclesiastes 3:1 we read, "For everything there is a season, and a time for every matter under heaven." There is a time for niceness, and a time for directness. How do you know which path to take in each situation?

As always, begin with prayer (see chapter 2). Through prayer the Holy Spirit will illuminate for you the right words to say and actions to take in each situation. Then you must allow your God-given intellect and common sense to guide you. And you should keep in mind four considerations when interacting with someone who rejects or ignores some aspect of the gospel.

First, how close is your relationship with that person? Are you a dear friend, a parent, a spouse, a fellow parishioner, or have you just met? Talking about the Faith with a longtime friend will differ greatly from doing so with someone you just met at your parish's Donut Sunday. Someone is much more likely to listen to criticism from a loyal friend than from a stranger. The closer we are to a person, the more direct we can be in how we talk and interact with him.

Second, for someone you know, consider his personality. Is he defensive? Does he take criticism well? This doesn't mean that you should refuse to confront someone who is thin-skinned, but how you do it may need to be adjusted. When I was considering Catholicism, my best friend, a Catholic, was very direct with me. He told me explicitly that I needed to convert and that some of my Protestant beliefs were heretical. I might have taken offense (and yes, I was annoyed at times), but he knew my personality, and knew that these direct statements would not turn me away.

A third consideration is the seriousness of the other person's sin or error. I have a devout Protestant friend from high school who loves Jesus, is a devoted husband, and is heavily involved in his children's lives. Many of his theological views align with Catholicism. To a great extent, he lives like a Catholic. With him, there is little need to be confrontational; instead, I try merely to explain Catholicism, display its beauty, and show him how it is the fulfillment of what he is already living. Another friend who lives a homosexual lifestyle is, however, a different story. He needs to confront some hard truths if he is to convert; my call may be to challenge him with those truths.

The fourth and final consideration relates to your role in the life of the other person. A parent or a priest has a far greater responsibility than a coworker. That doesn't mean you don't care about the salvation of your coworkers, but your role in bringing them to heaven will differ from that of the person's close relatives. Each of us plays different parts in the lives of those around us. I have met many parents whose adult children have fallen away from the Church. They are desperate to know what they should say or do to help bring their children back. I usually ask them, first, if their child knows how they feel about his or her life decisions. Invariably, they answer, "Oh yes, he knows we want him to return to the Church." Then I tell them something very hard for them to hear: in most situations, parents should stop trying to drag their child back into the Church. Instead, they should continue to pray for the child and ask the saints (especially St. Monica) to intercede for him. All too often, parents, in their frustration, resort to nagging the child at every opportunity: "Have you been to Mass lately?" "Are you still living with your girlfriend?" "When was the last time you went to confession?" The sheer repetition only makes the child deaf to these pleas. So, while always living the Faith themselves, parents might need to take a step back.

But other roles call for different responses. I remember some great advice a priest once gave right before the baptism of one of my children. He was talking to the godparents and told them, "You have one job: to help this child get to heaven. There may come a time in the future, God forbid, when she leaves the Church. If that happens, her parents might not be able to say anything—they may have too much baggage in their relationship to be effective. But as godparents you will have to confront her and urge her to return. Don't worry about your relationship with her—you are her godparents, and that is your only job." We all have different roles in the lives of people around us, and that will dictate whether we focus on "welcoming" them or confronting them in their sin or error.

Feeling Uncomfortable

Many of us are uncomfortable with confrontation. We're hesitant to be as direct as Jesus and many of the saints were. That's okay—God works with every personality. What's important is that we never allow ourselves to be "welcoming" toward sin or error.

When I was an Evangelical in college and heavily involved with the campus pro-life group, all of the dozen or so committed members of the group were Catholic except me. They were, of course, happy to have me as a member, and I always felt welcome as a fellow pro-lifer in the trenches. But being the only Protestant did sometimes make me uncomfortable, for they were unapologetic about their faith and their practice of it. When we went to an abortion clinic to pray, it was only a few moments before they pulled out their rosaries and began to pray their Hail Marys . . . while I stood off by myself, praying silently or reading my Bible. Sometimes they would invite me to Mass. When they did, they gently but firmly let me know that I was not invited to receive Communion.

Although I felt welcome as a person and as a full-fledged pro-lifer, there was always a barrier between us. They never gave any quarter to me in what they believed were my false beliefs—which bothered me, and even struck me as arrogance. "Who do they think they are? Do they think they're better than I am?" But in hindsight, I recognize that they were simply being faithful to their beliefs (beliefs I now share, of course). For them, faithfulness took precedence over making me feel comfortable.

And, in fact, my discomfort pushed me to study their beliefs and to discover why they held to them so strongly. In any conversion, discomfort is a necessity. Why would a person change his life if he's perfectly comfortable with it? Sometimes, by making others feel too welcome, we give them the impression that they're fine where they are, even if they hold erroneous beliefs or live a sinful lifestyle. When people feel a little uncomfortable, it's often because their consciences are being awakened.

But being willing to make others uncomfortable doesn't mean being a jerk. Our goal isn't to make people uncomfortable for its own sake. Some Catholics seem to think that the more in-your-face they are, the more faithful they are. But that may just be an overreaction to the excessively welcoming attitude that has become so prevalent in the Church. A simple guideline to follow is: always welcome the person, but never the sin or error.

Making Disciples

When it comes to evangelization, Christ gave us our marching orders in the Great Commission:

> All authority in heaven and on earth has been given to me. Go therefore and make disciples of all nations, baptizing them in the name of the Father and of the Son and of the Holy Spirit, teaching them to observe all that I have commanded you; and lo, I am with you always, to the close of the age (Matt. 28:18–20).

Notice: Christ enjoins us to make disciples, baptize people, and teach them his commands. Nowhere, however, does he say to "welcome" people. Again, the goal of evangelization is not "welcome," but *conversion*, for that is the essence of what Christ is calling for when he tasks us with making baptized disciples who will follow his commands.

Yes, welcome might be one *stage* in the process of making disciples, but it is not the final one. In fact, it is usually only the first one. When someone first approaches you about Catholicism—whether he's a longtime friend or a new acquaintance—you want to do all you can to make him feel comfortable. You don't want to turn him off. However, at some point the subject matter will get personal, and when things get personal, people usually get defensive. It is at this point that too many Catholics will avoid tough topics in a desire to remain "welcoming." But this is exactly where we most often fail in evangelization. In order to make disciples, we must be willing to push into uncomfortable areas—uncomfortable for us and for those whom we are evangelizing. Only by doing so will we dig below the surface and bring another to confront the Truth.

As we'll discuss in a later chapter, it's vital that we promote the sacrament of confession in our evangelization efforts. But telling someone he needs to go to confession—and, in effect, telling him he's a sinner—can come across as terribly unwelcoming. Yet if we never urge people to find reconciliation with Christ in this beautiful sacrament, for fear of turning them away, are we really doing our job of "making disciples" (Matt. 28:19)? Yes, some people may be offended and turn away from us. But Jesus said, "There will be more joy in heaven over one sinner who repents than over ninety-nine righteous persons who need no repentance" (Luke 15:7).

Too often we tell ourselves that being welcoming and being faithful are mutually exclusive. They are not. Let me tell you about two parishes, St. Jude and St. Rose. They were located about twenty miles apart. St. Jude was a large parish in an affluent suburb, with a popular pastor. The parish emphasized "welcoming" and underemphasized Catholic teaching. In many respects St. Jude was no different from a mainline Protestant church. Many Catholics praised it as a model of evangelization. But in my interactions with parishioners there, I found that almost without exception they dissented from various Church teachings and felt no need to work for the conversion of others to Catholicism; indeed, most of them felt it was better for non-Catholics to remain in whatever religion (or non-religion) they were currently in.

Contrast that with St. Rose parish. It was in a less affluent part of town, but it was bursting at the seams. The pastor was known in the community for being a staunch defender of Church teaching, especially in such controversial areas as abortion and sexual morality. But he was as beloved—if not more so—than the pastor of St. Jude. I found the parishioners at St. Rose to be as staunchly Catholic as their pastor and to fervently desire bringing others into the Church. Never did I find a warmer welcome than at St. Rose.

Which parish—St. Jude or St. Rose—was being faithful to Christ's call to make disciples who observe everything he commanded?

No inherent dichotomy exists between being welcoming to others and being faithful to Church teaching. We must always remember that being welcomed is only a step in the process of conversion, not the end goal. When Jesus confronted the Pharisees and lawyers, he did it in hopes of their conversion. His words might have been "unwelcoming," but he spoke them in order to eventually welcome them to eternal life with him.

Example

St. Polycarp

Polycarp was the bishop of Smyrna (in modern-day Turkey) in the second century. He has a direct connection to the apostles, for he was a disciple of St. John the Evangelist.

Polycarp is also one of the most famous martyrs of the early Church; the *Martyrdom of Polycarp* is a classic apologetic text that defends the Christian martyrs against the slanders of the Roman rulers of the time.

At his trial, Polycarp, then an old man, was asked to deny Christ. He responded, "Eighty and six years I have served him, and he has done me no wrong. How then can I blaspheme my King and Savior? You threaten me with a fire that burns for a season, and after a little while is quenched; but you are ignorant of the fire of everlasting punishment that is prepared for the wicked." When they bound Polycarp to the stake and lit the fire, the flames miraculously would not touch him, so they had to stab him in order to end his life.

As one might guess from his words at his execution, Polycarp was never afraid of speaking the truth. The most famous example of this was his encounter with the heretic Marcion. Marcion lived in Rome and was one of the most famous men of his day. He preached a mix of Christian and Gnostic beliefs, and believed that the Old Testament God was not the same as the God of Jesus Christ. He rejected most of the New Testament writings, and instead concocted his own scriptural canon from, among other things, snippets of the Gospel of Luke and the writings of St. Paul. His heretical teachings became very popular, gaining him many followers.

One day Polycarp was in Rome and happened by Marcion in the street. The arch-heresiarch, perturbed that Polycarp seemed not to recognize him, asked Polycarp, "Do you know me?" Polycarp answered,

"Yes, I know you, the firstborn of Satan." Not exactly words of welcome! But Polycarp knew that Marcion was leading many souls astray, and he had no desire to let that pass. In Polycarp's view, the most loving thing to do—for both Marcion and his deluded followers—was to oppose Marcion to his face.

We might never be called to label someone the offspring of the devil; neither, however, will we ever be called to welcome sin—but only to work for the conversion of sinners.

Examination

- Do I avoid confrontation at all costs in order to make sure others feel welcome at my parish?

- Do I see Jesus primarily as a gentle, mild man who never offended anyone?

Exploration

- Why do you think "welcoming" has replaced evangelization in many parishes?

- What is the proper role of "welcoming" in the context of evangelization?

- What do you think Jesus meant when he said, "I have come to bring division" (Luke 12:51)?

Exercise

- Most of us are close to someone who is living in a way contrary to the gospel. In prayer, resolve to address this irregular situation with him or her.

- The next time your parish priest publicly defends one of the Church's controversial teachings, let him know you appreciate it.

- Read the Gospel of Matthew. Note all the times Jesus says something challenging that might have made the people around him uncomfortable.

Overcoming
Doubts

4

Jesus Sometimes Fails
to Bring About Conversion

You're convinced of the importance of evangelization. You have decided to devote more time to prayer. You're excited to get going and start winning converts! You can picture your friends and family members being received into the Church at the Easter Vigil.

But what if you fail? What if, instead of converting, your loved ones reject your message—and maybe even reject you?

Everyone fears failure. Sometimes that fear can lead to paralysis: we don't do what we should because we're afraid we'll be unsuccessful. When it comes to personal relationships, the fear of failure—such as lost friendships, confrontations, or bad reputation—can keep us from evangelizing. We may rationalize our inaction, but the truth is that fear is keeping us from living our baptismal promise to share the gospel.

Encounter

The encounter with the rich young man (Matt. 19:16–22)

[16]And behold, one came up to him, saying, "Teacher, what good deed must I do, to have eternal life?" [17]And he said to him, "Why do you ask me about what is good? One there is who is good. If you would enter life, keep the commandments." [18]He said to him,

"Which?" And Jesus said, "You shall not kill, You shall not commit adultery, You shall not steal, You shall not bear false witness, [19]Honor your father and mother, and, You shall love your neighbor as yourself." [20]The young man said to him, "All these I have observed; what do I still lack?" [21]Jesus said to him, "If you would be perfect, go, sell what you possess and give to the poor, and you will have treasure in heaven; and come, follow me." [22]When the young man heard this he went away sorrowful; for he had great possessions.

Keeping the Relationship

"I'm afraid I'll harm our relationship—she'll never talk to me again."

I was talking to Laurie, and she was telling me about her sister Melissa, who was living with her boyfriend. Laurie wanted to talk to Melissa about the problems of this arrangement but was afraid Melissa would push her away if she did. Laurie loved her sister dearly and had been saddened when Melissa stopped going to Mass a few years before.

Her concern—that telling someone something she doesn't want to hear will lead to rejection—is one I hear often when talking to people about evangelization. As Laurie explained it, "If I tell my sister that living with her boyfriend is harmful, even sinful, she'll probably just tune me out and might even stop talking to me. But if I don't tell her, then perhaps over time I'll be able to bring her closer to God." The intention is good, but the logic is faulty.

My advice to Laurie was the same I've given many other people in similar circumstances. I told her that she can't predict or control her sister's reaction, but she can control her own words and actions. If she had demonstrated love for her sister over the years (and I'm sure she had), then Melissa would surely be mindful of that when Laurie told her something she found uncomfortable. Furthermore, Laurie couldn't count on anyone else talking to Melissa; after all, most people wouldn't see a problem with her behavior, and even if they did, they would probably, like Laurie, be afraid to say anything about it. Finally, Laurie had a certain obligation to Melissa as her sister that others—friends, coworkers, acquaintances—did not have. I also told her that the conversation most likely wouldn't be as bad as she was imagining.

Laurie decided to take my advice, and screwed up her courage to talk to her sister. She later told me it went "well" (meaning, most likely, that no dishes were thrown or cutlery abused), but Melissa didn't change her living situation. More than a year after Laurie talked to Melissa, there was no noticeable change in Melissa's lifestyle, or in Laurie and Melissa's relationship. In terms of Laurie's desired outcome, she had "failed." Does this mean she wasn't being faithful to Christ? Or was her "failure" more Christlike than she realized?

The Failure of One Who Is Perfect

The story of Christ's encounter with the rich young man is one of my favorites in all the Bible. We have this earnest young man, who both desires to go deeper in his spiritual life and sees Jesus as one who can lead him there. For any evangelist, it's the perfect combination! Spiritual apathy is all too common today—most people simply don't care about the spiritual life, making the job of the evangelist a steep uphill climb. The answer to the question "Do you think God exists?" is more often, in effect, "I don't care" than "yes" or "no."

But that's not the case with the rich young man. He approaches Jesus and asks the only question that really matters: "What good deed must I do, to have eternal life?" Here is someone who at an early age possesses all that the world has to offer: money and power (the parallel story in Luke 18:18–30 refers to him as a "ruler"). Yet he knows in his heart that these things are not enough to satisfy him. So he approaches someone he believes can show him a better, deeper satisfaction. If there was ever an ideal situation for an evangelist, this is it.

We see that Jesus does not begin by trying to "close the sale." First he simply repeats what any rabbi at the time would have said: "If you would enter life, keep the commandments." Even though it appears that this young man is serious about the spiritual life, Jesus wants to be sure. For if the young man has been living a life of hedonism or materialism, then his question might be just an academic one. But if he is already striving to keep the commandments, then perhaps he is ready to hear the good news that Jesus is proclaiming.

The rich young man's answer shows his initial disappointment. He most likely had been told about Jesus and his teachings, which is why he approached him. He expected some answer that would go deeper, to the heart of the spiritual life. To Jesus' instruction to "keep the commandments," he dutifully responds, "Which?" After Jesus lists the basic ones, the young man says, "All these I have observed; what do I still lack?" Can't you see him waving Jesus' answer aside with an impatient gesture? It's as if he's rebuking Jesus—"I heard you were a great spiritual teacher, but all you do is list the commandments. Any scribe or Pharisee could do that!" Jesus, however, has set him up. The young man is proud of being a practicing Jew, though he knows down deep that there is more to the spiritual life than just following the commandments. Jesus shows him just how much more: "If you would be perfect, go, sell what you possess and give to the poor, and you will have treasure in heaven; and come, follow me."

I can only guess what went through the young man's head at this point. What kind of answer was he expecting? Perhaps he thought Jesus would tell him about some new form of prayer, or explain some teaching from the Torah in a new and exciting way. In every age people want to make the spiritual life something separate and distinct from everyday life; to put it in modern terms, what you do from Monday through Saturday is unrelated to what you do on Sunday. Most likely the young man did not think his day-to-day life would need to change very much to obtain eternal life—after all, he kept the commandments! Yet Christ demands that the young man give up *everything* in order to "be perfect."

The young man's reaction is one of the most poignant, and tragic, in all of Scripture: "When the young man heard this he went away sorrowful; for he had great possessions." In the Gospels, we see Jesus healing the sick, performing great miracles, putting the learned Pharisees and Sadducees in their place. Yet here we see Jesus failing. As the perfect Son of God, his answer to this young man is as perfect as his answer to the Pharisees and Herodians about paying taxes to Caesar (Matt. 22:15–22). We delight when Jesus outsmarts proud religious leaders, but what do we think when he fails to convert someone who was clearly open to conversion?

Overcoming the Fear of Failure

Here are some of the most common objections I have heard in my years of evangelizing:

"We can't do that; it might upset people in the parish."

"We have to meet people where they are."

"If we do that, no one will come."

"I'm afraid I'll hurt our relationship if I say that to him."

In every case, what is feared is failure. And that fear of failure most often leads to a dilution and even alteration of our core message. This is essentially what mainstream Protestant denominations have done in recent decades. Their guiding principle has been to please people, not preach the gospel to them. So they water it down to make it more acceptable. No doubt their intentions are good, but in saying only what someone wants to hear, instead of what he *needs* to hear, they fail to effect true conversions.

I think most of us succumb to this temptation at times. How many of us have family members who have left the Church, whom we hesitate to challenge because we don't want to "harm the relationship"? How many of us avoid certain controversial topics, such as contraception, with fellow parishioners for fear of driving them away? We imagine all the ways we might offend others, and then choose to stay silent. But we do this on the basis of two false presuppositions: (1) that we know how the other person will react; and (2) that rejection would be proof that we shouldn't have spoken up. Let's look at each false presupposition in turn.

Are would-be evangelists mind readers? Well, many of us act like it. Laurie was *sure* that if she confronted Melissa about her lifestyle, Melissa would take offense and might never talk to her again. People too often hesitate to talk to someone about the gospel because they are absolutely *sure* they know how the person will react, and that it will be *badly*. I confess I've often given in to such fears. "She'll laugh at me." "He's going to think I'm a religious nut." "She won't talk to me anymore if I say that." But the fact is, *none* of us can know how people will react when we talk with them about the Faith. One thing that continually surprises me about my years of evangelization is how often I am wrong. I've never seen as bad a reaction as I've imagined in my head. The first time I went door-to-door for my parish, inviting strangers to visit our church and learn more about the Catholic faith, I was sure I would encounter slammed doors, rudeness, and perhaps even threats. Yet nothing like that ever happened. What I encountered instead were open minds, genuine interest, and thoroughly polite expressions of "no thanks." None of the people I met were like the anti-Catholic monsters of my imagination.

But what if you *are* rejected? What if presenting the truths of the gospel to someone harms your relationship with him? Here again we can learn from the encounter of Jesus and the rich young man. Jesus confronted this man about his root sin—his attachment to possessions—and the result was that Christ "harmed their relationship;" specifically, the young man walked away from Jesus, probably never to return. With his foreknowledge and divine power, of course, Christ actually *could* read minds; yet he still gave this soul the freedom to respond rightly. He didn't allow the possibility of rejection to change his message or prevent him from delivering it.

What Is Success?

Some readers might be dismayed when I write that our Lord "failed" in his encounter with the rich young man. How can the divine Son of God ever fail? The answer, of course, is that he can't. Christ "failed" only according to worldly standards. Just as his crucifixion made him seem a failure to most men, it was actually a great heavenly success; so too was his exchange with the rich young man ultimately a success.

Accordingly, the way to determine success in evangelization is not how people react to it; rather, our success is measured by how well we present the gospel message. A preacher as gifted as Fulton Sheen did not have 100-percent conversion rates—does that mean that he failed sometimes? Not necessarily. In any evangelization situation, the person being evangelized has free will, a unique personality, and a particular life situation. You might say the same thing to two people and meet with two radically different responses. We can only present the message; we cannot decide for the other person.

Ask these three questions of yourself to determine the "success" of your evangelization efforts:

1. Did I accurately represent the teachings of Christ and his Church?
   Note that there are two ways a person can be inaccurate in this: by stating something contrary to Church teaching, or by watering Church teaching down so much that it isn't properly conveyed.

2. Was I charitable in all I said and did?
   Being charitable means that you always assume the best about other people, and that you always want what is best for them. It doesn't mean being a pushover, but treating others as you want to be treated.

3. Did I invite the person to draw closer to Christ?
   Simply telling people about Jesus isn't enough: evangelization involves *inviting* them to make a change in their lives, to fully embrace Christ and his Church.

These are our standards for success—not the number of converts we gain.

A priest once told me the results of an interesting study. It found that by the time someone converts, he has already had over 150 "points of contact" with Catholicism. So, for example, a Protestant who becomes Catholic may have gone to a Catholic wedding, made friends with a Catholic co-worker, read a book that presents Catholicism in an appealing way, or met a priest on an airplane. All of these encounters might nudge him toward conversion, in ways he doesn't even recognize. Further, the Catholics who influenced him might never know this side of heaven that they did so.

I know this was true for my own conversion. Before I went off to college, I didn't have much interaction with practicing Catholics. In fact, my Bible study leaders in high school were a formerly Catholic couple who had become Evangelicals. When I joined the pro-life group in college, however, I discovered something new: Catholics (including my future wife) who were truly Christians while remaining Catholic! This affected me profoundly. Yet none of these people realized the influence they were having on me, or that it would eventually lead to my conversion. If they had intended to convert me, they surely would have believed they had failed, for I gave no indication that I wanted to become Catholic and in fact on numerous occasions explicitly denied any interest in converting (including just weeks before my actual conversion). Yet each of these Catholics was a successful evangelist.

Conversion is usually a gradual process that appears sudden only to those on the outside. In a way, it is 149 points of failure followed by one big success. Yet the Holy Spirit is using those 149 points of failure to bring about conversion. As evangelists, we can never know if we are one of the 149 points, or even will be *the* one that triggers conversion (the odds, clearly, are against it). So we must simply continue to evangelize, knowing that true success means being faithful to God's truth in proclaiming it to others.

Bottom line: If we evangelize enough, we are sure to experience "failure" in the form of rejection, indifference, and opposition. We've seen that even Christ sometimes "failed" in such a sense in his own evangelization efforts. But he calls us to evangelize anyway, concentrating on our message rather than tallying the results.

Example

St. Augustine of Canterbury

In the late sixth century St. Gregory the Great, at the time abbot of the monastery of St. Andrew's, noticed three fair-haired slaves at the market. He inquired as to their identity and was told they were "Angles" from the island of Great Britain. He responded, "Not angles, but angels!" Thus began the future pope's fascination with the people of England. He became a missionary to the island, having obtained permission from Pope Pelagius II to go there with a small band of fellow monks. But the people of Rome wanted Gregory for themselves and forced him to return—which, however, did not diminish his desire that the "Angles" be evangelized, and when he became the supreme pontiff, he found a way.

Pope St. Gregory selected a group of around forty monks from his former monastery to become missionaries to Great Britain. He named Augustine their leader. On their way to England, the band heard rumors of the savageness of the English, and sent Augustine back to Gregory for permission to abandon the mission. But

Gregory persuaded Augustine to continue with it, and so the missionary group did.

Upon their arrival, Augustine was met by King Ethelbert from the royal city of Canterbury. Ethelbert was unimpressed with Augustine's preaching, and showed no interest in the Catholic faith. This was a disheartening failure for Augustine, since in those days converting the king was usually the first step toward converting the nation. Ethelbert did, however, allow Augustine and his band to stay in England and do as they pleased. The small group of monks traveled extensively throughout the island, working to convert its inhabitants, but with little success.

Eventually, Ethelbert came to appreciate Augustine's gentle ways, holy life, and teachings. He asked to receive instruction in Catholicism, and on Christmas Day, 597, he, along with ten thousand of his subjects, were baptized by the monks, led by Augustine, who that same day became the first archbishop of Canterbury. Even though Augustine initially got no positive response to his evangelization efforts in England, in time they bore fruit in the conversion of an entire nation to Christ and his Church.

Examination

- Do I fear that I might lose a friend if I push my faith too much?

- Do I look only to visible results when considering the success of my evangelization efforts?

Exploration

- Other than in his encounter with the rich young man, what are some times Christ "failed" to bring about a conversion, or even drove people away by his words?

- Why do we fear failure so much?

- Why is it inaccurate to call Christ's encounter with the rich young man a failure?

Exercise

- Think of some previous "failure" you have had in evangelization. Resolve to pray for the people involved, and thank God for the opportunity to experience rejection in his name.

- If you've had an idea for an evangelization project that you've avoided doing because you fear it will fail, determine to move forward with it, asking God for help that you might be faithful in your work.

- Read the account of St. Paul at the Areopagus (Acts 17:16–34). Consider how he failed in his mission, but also succeeded.

5

Jesus Makes the Impossible Possible

The job of the Catholic evangelist can be a frustrating one. When we think about how far some of our friends and loved ones are from God, maintaining hope for their conversion is difficult. Perhaps we see no fruit from our efforts. Eventually we're tempted to simply accept the situation and move on. We believe it's impossible for them to convert.

But we must persevere and trust God to *do* the impossible. Christ said, "With men this is impossible, but with God all things are possible" (Matt. 19:26). The conversion of the most hardened sinner or skeptic *is* possible—and God greatly desires for it to happen. As we meet with seemingly insurmountable obstacles in our evangelizing, let's have faith that God can do anything, if we trust in him.

Encounter

The raising of Jairus's daughter (Luke 8:40–56)

[40]Now when Jesus returned, the crowd welcomed him, for they were all waiting for him. [41]And there came a man named Jairus, who was a ruler of the synagogue; and falling at Jesus' feet he besought him to come to his house, [42]for he had an only daughter, about twelve years of age, and she was dying.

As he went, the people pressed round him. [43]And a woman who had had a flow of blood for twelve years and had spent all her living upon physicians, and could not be healed by anyone [44]came up behind him, and touched the fringe of his garment; and immediately her flow of blood ceased. [45]And Jesus said, "Who was it that touched me?" When all denied it, Peter said, "Master, the multitudes surround you and press upon you!" [46]But Jesus said, "Some one touched me; for I perceive that power has gone forth from me." [47]And when the woman saw that she was not hidden, she came trembling, and falling down before him declared in the presence of all the people why she had touched him, and how she had been immediately healed. [48]And he said to her, "Daughter, your faith has made you well; go in peace."

[49]While he was still speaking, a man from the ruler's house came and said, "Your daughter is dead; do not trouble the Teacher any more." [50]But Jesus on hearing this answered him, "Do not fear; only believe, and she shall be well." [51]And when he came to the house, he permitted no one to enter with him, except Peter and John and James, and the father and mother of the child. [52]And all were weeping and bewailing her; but he said, "Do not weep; for she is not dead but sleeping." [53]And they laughed at him, knowing that she was dead. [54]But taking her by the hand he called, saying, "Child, arise." [55]And her spirit returned, and she got up at once; and he directed that something should be given her to eat. [56]And her parents were amazed; but he charged them to tell no one what had happened.

Addressing the Elephant in the Room

Like so many other cradle Catholics, my friend Diane stopped practicing her Catholic faith during college. But she never stopped believing in God and considered herself a Christian, and she eventually became involved in a Protestant young adult group. She began dating Steve, a Protestant who was also active in the group, and within a few years they were married in an Episcopal service. Diane appeared destined to be a permanent part of that large group of cradle Catholics who became "fallen away."

After many years, however, Diane developed a yearning to return to the Church of her youth. Steve had no objection, so they began attending Sunday Mass. She had no idea that her marriage was invalid (a Catholic must be married in a Catholic church unless a specific dispensation is given), and ignorantly received Communion. Then one day her pastor, Fr. Andrews, preached a homily that suggested to her that her marriage might not be valid. She was shocked: like so many modern Catholics, she had been woefully catechized and had little knowledge of the Church's teachings or its rules regarding marriage.

So she set up a meeting with Fr. Andrews to discuss the issue. In a situation like this, many priests and laypeople take a "say nothing to upset the person or turn him away" approach: they obfuscate the issue at hand, or flatly contradict what the Church teaches, in an effort to keep the person in the Church. A priest once told me that he never wants to turn someone away from the Church, so he tries to avoid any topic that he thinks might be alienating. He's not simply trying to avoid confrontation or conflict, he said; he believes this is an effective evangelization method. So in a case such as Diane's, he—and others like him—might conclude that telling her that her marriage is presumptively invalid would be erecting an insurmountable barrier to her return to the Church. The underlying assumption is that it's inconceivable that the message would be accepted.

Fortunately for Diane, however, Fr. Andrews did not subscribe to this philosophy. Believing that "the truth will set you free" (John 8:32, NAB), he clearly and gently told Diane the true status of her marriage. No doubt he was uncomfortable, and it took no small amount of courage to be honest with her. I can just imagine how he struggled inwardly as he told Diane something no Catholic would want to hear. But Fr. Andrews believed that with God all things are possible, and he trusted the Lord to soften her heart.

Diane was understandably dismayed. How could the Church say that her marriage was not valid? One might guess that she went away angry and, once again, abandoned the Faith. But no, grace was at work. And in fact, she researched on her own what the Church teaches about marriage, accepted those teachings, and undertook steps to correct her irregular situation, meanwhile refraining from Holy Communion.

Eventually Diane and Steve had their marriage convalidated by the Church, and she became a daily communicant. Steve, by the way, after many years of marriage—and of raising their children as Catholics—entered the Church himself. One factor in his conversion was the Church's uncompromising affirmation of the sanctity and the indissolubility of marriage. Although they have since moved away from the area, Diane and Steve keep in contact with Fr. Andrews and consider him in many ways their spiritual father.

When Diane first came to Fr. Andrews, he faced a choice: either assume that the barrier to change was too great and hide the truth from her, or gently confront her and Steve with the Church's teachings, having faith that Christ could bring them to a total acceptance of that truth. Fr. Andrews chose faith over doubt—faith that Christ could do the impossible. Christ's encounter with Jairus shows us the wisdom of Fr. Andrews's course of action.

The Faith of Jairus

Jairus is faced with a terrible situation: the impending death of his twelve-year-old daughter. He's willing to consider anything that might bring her back to health. In the normal course of affairs, Jairus, whom Luke calls a "ruler," surely would not want to be involved with someone of such dubious reputation as Jesus, much less be indebted to him. Yet he has heard stories of this supposed wonder worker, and if even the least of these tales is true, perhaps it is possible. . . . So this venerable ruler prostrates himself before Jesus and asks the only thing in the world he wants at that moment: for his beloved daughter not to die.

Jesus indicates that he's willing at least to see the girl, but his popularity makes it difficult for him even to walk from town to town—all the people want to see him, to touch him, to hear some words of wisdom or comfort from him. So the going is slow to Jairus's house. Imagine the frustration building in the ruler's heart: Don't people realize that this is an emergency? Doesn't *Jesus* realize it is an emergency? Yet the people still come, including the woman with the flow of blood who was healed just by touching Christ's cloak.

But then Jairus sees one of his servants approaching, his face long, unable to look his master in the eye. Jairus knows instantly what this means: he's too late. Even if Jesus is a wonder worker as the people say, he cannot raise his daughter from the dead. His servant confirms the worst: "Your daughter is dead; do not trouble the Teacher any more." Surely the servant's heart is in the right place, for why make a show of Jesus coming to the house when nothing can be done? Would it not be the height of cruelty to encourage hope when there is none to be had?

But wait.

On hearing the servant Jesus replies, "Do not fear; only believe, and she shall be well."

What can this mean? Either Jesus didn't hear the servant correctly, or else he's crazy: everyone knows that only God has power over life and death—who is this man who thinks he can overcome death? But Jairus is gripped by a desperation that only the parent of a dying child can know. If there is any hope, any hope at all, what would it hurt just to let Jesus see the girl? Perhaps, just perhaps . . .

So Jesus enters Jairus's house and says to the girl, "Child, arise." At these two simple words, Luke tells us, "her spirit returned, and she got up at once." The impossible is possible, after all.

This lesson—that what appears to us to be impossible is in fact possible for God—has profound implications for evangelization. It tells us that we must set our sights high when we present the gospel to others—every person can receive salvation and be transformed, no matter his current state in life. Christ's gift of salvation is offered for *all* people, without exception. The way of life he teaches is possible for *all* people, regardless of their background or previous lifestyle. As evangelists proclaiming the gospel, we cannot consider any person, or any situation, beyond the power of God's grace.

The Heresy of Low Expectations

Like prayer, belief in the impossible separates evangelization from mere marketing. When a corporation wishes to sell a product, it doesn't assume that the product is for everyone and should be marketed to everyone. Instead it does intensive research to see who would most need or want the product. A smart corporation doesn't try to sell the latest technological gadget to an Amish community; nor does it pitch an economy car to wealthy people. It understands there are limits on what one can sell, and to whom. But in evangelization there are no such limits—if we trust that "what is impossible with man is possible with God" (Luke 18:37).

The conviction that all people—and all lifestyles—can be transformed by Christ is especially needed today as we deal with issues of sex and marriage. So many Catholics, like Diane, find themselves in "irregular marriages"—unions that are recognized by the state but not the Church. Often these unions have lasted for decades and produced children, so calling the unions "invalid" seems harsh indeed. Or consider the case of a young person with same-sex attraction. Many would say that it is too much to ask of him that he live chastely for the rest of his life; the sex drive is simply too strong, and besides, it's unfair that heterosexuals can enjoy sex but not homosexuals.

Another example: a woman who is divorced and remarried without an annulment. How can we tell her she must live as "brother and sister" with her second spouse if she wishes to receive Communion? Isn't such a demand impossible in the "real world"? Isn't it to ask for more than is humanly possible—as did those scribes and Pharisees whom Christ condemned as placing on others "heavy burdens, hard to bear" (Matt. 23:4)?

This is the heresy of low expectations.

"We can't ask them to live chastely, that's just not possible."

"We'll never outlaw abortion; we just need to reduce how many abortions are committed."

"Asking people to attend Mass on Sundays *plus* holy days of obligation is just too much. We should reduce the days they need to go."

"We can't offer adoration at our parish—no one will come."

Low expectations is a "heresy" of sorts because it contradicts the teaching and example of the Gospels.

Look at the expectation that Christ sets for his followers in Matthew 5:48: "You, therefore, must be perfect, as your heavenly Father is perfect!" Note also the context of this radical statement: the Sermon on the Mount, in which Christ raised the standard of moral teaching for his followers from what was given to Moses for the Jewish people. He said we have to turn the other cheek, cannot divorce, and have to love our enemies: all things that sometimes appear humanly impossible. And the audience for the Sermon on the Mount was not limited to a select group of his followers, such as the apostles. Instead, the audience was *all* his followers, no matter their situation in life. His demand that we strive for perfection, then, is for everyone.

In our desire to bring people into the Church, evangelists can be tempted to remove any hurdle that might slow the process down. So when a couple comes to church and we learn that they're in an invalid marriage, we look the other way, afraid to say something that will upset them. When an engaged couple comes looking to get married, we ignore the fact that they're already living together. If we did attempt, for example, to show them that premarital cohabitation can be destructive to married life, it might offend them and send them straight to the local courthouse for a civil marriage. Down deep we don't think it's possible for people to change, or that they will want to change. This is to sell them a mess of pottage, however, while their birthright as sons and daughters of God demands that we give them the chance to respond to God's grace.

What if no priest ever preached a sermon to Diane and Steve that explained what constitutes a valid Catholic marriage? What if no one told Diane that her marriage was not recognized by the Church? Instead of the brief distress she would have felt, she might have lived for years, perhaps decades, in violation of the moral precepts given to Christ's followers, and blocked from many of the graces that Christ desired to give her. In addition, the witness of the gravity with which the Church treats marriage would have been lost on Steve, and most likely he would never have entered the Church. In the end, confronting Diane with the truth—and trusting Christ to give her the grace necessary to live that truth—was the most charitable thing someone could do for her, and it led to a family drawn closer to Christ. And this is, after all, the purpose of evangelization.

Transforming Mercy

Today's Catholic typically focuses on the mercy of God rather than on his justice, and rightly so: God's mercy is infinite and can never be fully appreciated. Yet we too often mistake the nature of his mercy. Looking the other way while people live in sin because it would be "too hard" for them to escape it is not mercy—it's cruelty. Often we are like Jairus's servant: "Don't trouble the Lord because he can't do anything about this situation." But in reality it is we who do not want to be troubled, by having to make the sacrifices necessary—such as unceasing prayer, fasting, and confrontation—to affect change in a loved one's life. So we consign others to a life not fully alive in God's grace.

I once heard a priest say, "I want to be a lion from the pulpit and a lamb in the confessional." Precisely! We must call people to live in accordance with God's law, but always extend them God's mercy when they fall. But too many of us want to be a lamb from our own pulpits—the sphere of influence in which we find ourselves—never exhorting people to a better life. But a lamb in the pulpit leads to no one in the confessional—for sin will simply be ignored.

We manifest a certain arrogance and conceit when we lower the bar for those who live in sin. Do we who are striving to live by God's law believe we're so special that we can do it, but others can't? Do we think God has chosen us to live this way, but not others? Those who have seen the grace of God work in their own lives should be inspired to help others receive that same grace, so that they too can work to conform to God's law.

Those who are willing—and courageous enough—to trust God to work miracles see wonderful results. Look at the Catholic apostolate Courage, which ministers to people suffering from same-sex attraction. While acknowledging that the causes of same-sex attraction are complex and often deep-seated, Courage nonetheless calls men and women with this affliction to live chastely. Many souls have heeded this call and found healing and peace. But Courage has been reviled and rejected for this work by many people, perhaps no more so than by Catholics who believe that people with same-sex attraction cannot change their behavior.

One member of Courage I know told me that he tried for years to get a Courage chapter started in his diocese but was opposed by the local bishop, who told him that he didn't believe that people with same-sex attraction could leave the homosexual lifestyle. What an indictment of that bishop's lack of faith—one shared by too many Catholics. As evangelizers, we must believe in the depths of our hearts that Christ can do anything. If he can raise someone from the dead, why can't he give someone the strength to overcome a deep-seated disorder and to reject temptation, no matter how strong?

As Catholic evangelists we must resist setting our sights low. While recognizing the reality of sin, we must call people to the great adventure of a life completely given over to Christ. There is no mercy in allowing a person to wallow in his sins; instead, the greatest mercy is to challenge him to confront his sins and abandon himself to God. Impossible as it may seem, we know that the One who raised Jairus's daughter from the dead can raise any sinful man or woman into a life of grace.

Example

St. Monica

Many Catholic mothers today experience what is perhaps their worst nightmare: a child who has abandoned the Faith and is living a profligate lifestyle. The pain, guilt, and frustration can be overwhelming, and despair is a frequent temptation. The belief that even God can't restore that child's faith stalks one's thoughts day and night. St. Monica could have easily fallen into this kind of despair: her son, Augustine, was an important person in the Roman Empire but had abandoned the Catholic faith in which he was raised. He lived only for himself.

Imagine if St. Monica had decided that her son's promiscuous lifestyle was too hard for him to escape, as he himself asserted. But she knew that a richer life was possible for her licentious son. So she prayed unceasingly for him, assuming a very important truth many forget: that God can do *anything*. And she didn't pray in a perfunctory fashion. No, she practically demanded that God save her son, and she backed it up with very concrete actions (that today would be considered "extreme"). Her prayer was answered, and how wonderfully! Her son became one of our greatest saints and a Doctor of the Church. Were the young Augustine alive today, would we be content to let him wallow in his sinful lifestyle, looking for "positive values" in his immoral relationships? Or would we, like St. Monica, trust that God can make the seemingly impossible possible?

Examination

- Do I know someone who has left the Faith? Do I despair that he can ever return?

- Do I think a family member's "alternative" lifestyle is the best that she can achieve?

Exploration

- What is the "heresy of low expectations"? Why is it a heresy of sorts?

- What does it mean to be a "lion from the pulpit and a lamb in the confessional"? How does this apply to laymen?

- How can Jairus's love for his daughter be a model for us in evangelization?

Exercise

- Make a list of people you have "written off" for conversion. Begin to pray for them daily and consider concrete steps to evangelize them.

- Look into starting a Courage chapter in your diocese. If one already exists, promote it in your parish and your community.

- Imagine yourself as Ananias (see Acts 9). How would you react if Saul—the persecutor of Christians—came to your house? Would you believe he could convert?

Joining the
Battle

6

Jesus Confronts the Devil

When we begin to evangelize, we enter into a battle—a battle for souls. In that battle, who's our enemy? Clearly not the people we're trying to convert. Rather, it's the spiritual forces that desire to keep people in sin and darkness. If we don't recognize this, we won't be successful in our evangelization efforts.

Being Catholic entails belief in the spiritual world. We're quick to embrace that belief when thinking about guardian angels or living forever in heaven. But when talk of the spiritual world turns to such uncomfortable subjects as demons or spending eternity in hell, many of us clam up—these subjects are simply too far outside our comfort zone. We avoid talking about them either because we don't believe that a loving God could allow such things, or because we believe other people will think we're crazy and reject us.

Yet Jesus confronted the demonic head-on and warned his followers continually of the possibility of hell for those who reject him. Are we willing to confront demonic forces in our efforts to save people from hell?

Encounter

The battle with the Gerasene demoniac (Mark 5:1–20)

¹They came to the other side of the sea, to the country of the Gerasenes. ²And when he had come out of the

boat, there met him out of the tombs a man with an unclean spirit, [3]who lived among the tombs; and no one could bind him any more, even with a chain; [4]for he had often been bound with fetters and chains, but the chains he wrenched apart, and the fetters he broke in pieces; and no one had the strength to subdue him. [5]Night and day among the tombs and on the mountains he was always crying out, and bruising himself with stones. [6]And when he saw Jesus from afar, he ran and worshiped him; [7]and crying out with a loud voice, he said, "What have you to do with me, Jesus, Son of the Most High God? I adjure you by God, do not torment me." [8]For he had said to him, "Come out of the man, you unclean spirit!" [9]And Jesus asked him, "What is your name?" He replied, "My name is Legion; for we are many." [10]And he begged him eagerly not to send them out of the country. [11]Now a great herd of swine was feeding there on the hillside; [12]and they begged him, "Send us to the swine, let us enter them." [13]So he gave them leave. And the unclean spirits came out, and entered the swine; and the herd, numbering about two thousand, rushed down the steep bank into the sea, and were drowned in the sea.

[14]The herdsmen fled, and told it in the city and in the country. And people came to see what it was that had happened. [15]And they came to Jesus, and saw the demoniac sitting there, clothed and in his right mind, the man who had had the legion; and they were afraid. [16]And those who had seen it told what had happened to the demoniac and to the swine. [17]And they began to beg Jesus to depart from their neighborhood. [18]And as he was getting into the boat, the man who had been possessed with demons begged him that he might be with

him. [19]But he refused, and said to him, "Go home to your friends, and tell them how much the Lord has done for you, and how he has had mercy on you." [20]And he went away and began to proclaim in the Decapolis how much Jesus had done for him; and all men marveled.

The Devil Made Them Do It

As I've mentioned, while in college I was actively involved with a pro-life group which gave me my first exposure to practicing Catholics. But it was also where I first directly encountered the power of the demonic. Each Friday afternoon our small group traveled about an hour to the nearest abortion clinic in order to pray there and to counsel women who were considering abortion. This was in the early 1990s, when Operation Rescue was at its height, and many thousands of pro-lifers were being arrested for blocking abortion clinic doors. So on most Fridays there was a police presence at the clinic. We typically arrived around 5 p.m. and stayed until the clinic closed at 6 p.m. Rain or shine, hot or cold, we felt it necessary to be there to intercede for the mothers and their babies. Most weeks it was relatively quiet, but in the weeks surrounding the January 22 anniversary of *Roe v. Wade*, rabid pro-abortion students from another local college would arrive to demonstrate against us.

One year, the Friday before January 22 was particularly crowded. About fifteen of our members attended, plus another twenty to thirty pro-lifers from the area. About the same number of pro-abortion advocates were also there. The police showed up to keep things in order. As usual, we prayed (I, being one of the few non-Catholics in our group, did not join in the usual Rosary, but prayed silently instead), and a few of our number tried to counsel women to keep their babies. At 6:00, the clinic staff began to leave, and so did most of the protesters and counter-protesters. But our college group stayed on and kept praying. Seeing this, the pro-abortion college students stayed, too. The police left, however, apparently assuming that with the clinic closed their job was done.

As practiced pro-lifers, we were used to jeers and taunts from pro-abortion folks. Contrary to the media stereotype, the typical pro-life protester remains in silent prayer when baited by counter-protesters. Also contrary to the media depiction, pro-abortion protestors are usually loud and obnoxious, chanting slogans such as "Not the church, not the state—women must decide their fate!" or "Keep your rosaries off my ovaries!" (this always gets a laugh when the chanter is male). In general, though, it's harmless stuff. But on this night, things got ugly.

As we gathered in a tight group to pray, the pro-aborts began to encircle us—at first silently, but eventually chanting, in an unearthly way, "Kill the Christians! Kill the Christians! Bring back the lions! Bring back the lions!" And this was not some ironic, half-joking chant—they were deadly serious. As the evening sky darkened, the pro-aborts' chants darkened as well, becoming more and more obscene and blasphemous about our Lord as well as the Blessed Virgin Mary (as a Protestant, I found that curious). At one point, I glanced up from my prayers and looked one of the pro-aborts in the eye. Though of course I can't prove it, I felt immediately that he was possessed by a demon. As I looked around at the rest of them, I realized that this is what our spiritual life is always like, with demonic forces—albeit invisible ones—relentlessly harassing and attacking us. As St. Peter wrote, "Your adversary the devil prowls around like a roaring lion, seeking some one to devour" (1 Pet. 5:8). This verse was no longer theoretical for me; I knew that the devil and his demons are real, and want our destruction.

Tempted by Satan

To some people, my story might sound outlandish and even sensationalistic. Aren't these just misguided college kids you're talking about? Do you really think they were *possessed*? Isn't your conclusion extreme? Such questions, I believe, may arise only because most people today deny the existence of demons.

When we read the Gospels, on the other hand, we see a very different perspective. Demonic forces are constantly in the background, and it's clear they're fighting to undermine Jesus and his mission. In fact, at the beginning of his public ministry, we see him going into the wilderness, where he is "tempted by Satan" (Mark 1:13). This establishes an underlying theme of all the Gospels: Jesus' mission is to confront Satan and to overthrow his kingdom.

Nowhere is this mission more explicit than with the encounter Jesus has with the "Gerasene demoniac" (Mark 5:1–20). Mark tells us that Jesus comes to "the country of the Gerasenes" and meets a man "with an unclean spirit." This poor soul lived among the tombs and was often bound with chains, to protect both himself and those around him. He was "always crying out, and bruising himself with stones." Many modern commentators offer a completely naturalistic explanation for this phenomenon, saying that the man was simply mentally unstable. Yet when this pitiful man encounters Jesus, the Lord immediately commands, "Come out of the man, you unclean spirit!" He sees the man's problems for what they really are: possession by a demonic spirit. When Jesus asks, "What is your name?" he is not asking the man's name, but the spirit's. The demon replies, "My name is Legion; for we are many." In other words, the man isn't possessed by just one demon, but by many. Yet they have no power over Christ, and the Lord drives them out of the man into a local herd of swine.

Compare an encounter like this, or my experience at the abortion clinic years ago, with life in a typical parish. Is there any acknowledgment there of a battle between our world and demonic forces? More specifically, in our efforts to bring people into (or back into) the Church do we acknowledge that there might be powerful forces arrayed against us—forces that wish to drive souls to hell?

One Hell of an Evangelist

Polls have shown that almost 70 percent of Americans believe in the existence of hell, but only a much smaller percentage believe that many, if any, people actually go there. And even among those who do believe that hell is well populated, few think that the possibility of eternal damnation should be part of the Church's evangelistic message. They argue for this "ignore hell" approach on the following grounds:

1. Modern Catholics don't respond to threats of hellfire and brimstone.
2. We should follow God not because we fear punishment, but because we love him.

But is it true that modern Catholics don't respond to threats of hellfire and brimstone? There is no way to know, since even the mention of hell has been banished from almost every Catholic parish in America. Other than "contraceptive," there is no word more unlikely to be heard from the parish pulpit. This may well account, at least in part, for why the Church's numbers have dropped precipitously. So how can we say that modern Catholics don't respond to threats of hellfire and brimstone? All we really know for sure is that they don't respond to promises of heaven for everyone. Otherwise our parishes would be full today.

So do Catholics avoid proclaiming the reality of hell because no one takes it seriously anymore, or does no one take hell seriously anymore because Catholics refuse to proclaim it?

What about the objection that we should follow God out of love rather than fear of punishment? True, obeying God out of love is better than obeying him out of fear. But the Church has always taught that obeying God out of fear is still sufficient to attain heaven and often leads to loving obedience. All good parents know that if the rules they set for their children have no punishments attached to them, the children will likely disobey. But if punishments *are* given for bad behavior, over time children will grow to understand the wisdom behind the rules and to obey their parents out of love. Although it is a modern conceit to consider ourselves too mature to need the threat of punishment, in the practice of the Faith we are like children. What we do first out of fear of punishment we may eventually do out of a loving understanding and acceptance of Catholicism's "rules."

On the surface, it might seem that talking about hell is antithetical to evangelization. After all, evangelization means "preaching the good news" and hell is the opposite of good news: "Good news! You might be consigned to unquenchable fire for all eternity!" Yet proclaiming the existence of hell—and the possibility that we could go there for eternity—is essential to preaching the "good news." Why? Because if there is nothing bad to avoid, then there is no need to take seriously the good news.

Jesus understood the importance of preaching the "bad news" along with the good. Although it is common today to see Jesus as a 1960s hippie philosopher who preaches only tolerance, inclusiveness, and ecumenical dialogue, the Gospels portray a teacher much given to issuing warnings about hell.

Three times in the Sermon on the Mount, Jesus warns that a certain sin will send someone to hell (Matt. 5:22, 29, 30). In many of his parables, the threat of hell is explicit: in the parable of the sheep and the goats (Matt. 25:31–46), for instance, those who didn't serve the poor and the needy are sent away into "eternal punishment"; and in the parable of the rich man and Lazarus (Luke 16:19–31), the rich man, having ignored the sufferings of Lazarus, finds himself in Hades, where he begs for just a drop of water, "for I am in anguish in this flame." In the Gospel of Matthew alone, Jesus mentions the "fire" of hell ten times as punishment for various sins.

Even in his "positive" teachings, Jesus warns of the negative consequences of denying them. For example, he proclaims, "I am the vine, you are the branches. He who abides in me, and I in him, he it is that bears much fruit" (John 15:5). What is often ignored is what our Lord says next: "If a man does not abide in me, he is cast forth as a branch and withers; and the branches are gathered, thrown into the fire and burned" (John 15:6). Also, Christ promises that "he who eats my flesh and drinks my blood has eternal life" (John 6:54), but only *after* he warns, "unless you eat the flesh of the Son of man and drink his blood, you have no life in you" (John 6:53).

For the early Christians, the idea that one must ignore hell in order to preach the good news was inconceivable. Consider this passage:

> John answered them all, "I baptize you with water; but he who is mightier than I is coming, the thong of whose

sandals I am not worthy to untie; he will baptize you with the Holy Spirit and with fire. His winnowing fork is in his hand, to clear his threshing floor, and to gather the wheat into his granary, but the chaff he will burn with unquenchable fire" (Luke 3:16–17).

What does Luke say about this uplifting message of burning in unquenchable fire? "So, with many other exhortations, he preached good news to the people" (Luke 3:18). Unlike in the modern pseudo-gospel—which sounds less like John's Gospel than like John Lennon's "Imagine"—the danger of hell was a core teaching in the early Church, and remained so until recent times. The possibility of hell for those who reject Christ has always been balanced by the promise of heaven for those who follow him. Today's Church must not only restore that balance, but must also warn about the many beliefs and actions approved of in our society that actually *put one on the path* to eternal separation from God. This does not mean that we have to lead with a discussion of hell, but we must not ignore it either. Warning about hell isn't any more "negative" than warning someone about the dangers of drowning.

Ultimately, properly proclaiming the good news doesn't ignore the existence of hell—it proclaims victory over it through the power of Christ's resurrection for those who follow him.

Engaging in Battle

What are some practical ways to follow Jesus' example in our battle against spiritual forces? The first is a mind-shift. Instead of seeing evangelization as a marketing outreach—trying to "sell" people on the Catholic Church—we need to see it as a pitched battle for souls. Let's recognize that the devil and his minions are working hard to prevent conversions. This leads to a second practical application: prayer. We're in a battle with forces far more powerful than we are, so we need to call in the reinforcements: our Lady, the saints, and the angels. If we try to evangelize without their help, we'll be doomed to failure. Finally, when evangelizing we should talk openly about the existence of dark spiritual forces and the possibility of hell. The devil made these topics uncomfortable to talk about, because he knows that he is most effective when hidden. But it is better for you to be uncomfortable now than for the people you care about to be much worse than uncomfortable for all eternity!

Too often Catholics are like the community of Gerasene. When we're confronted with the presence of the demonic, we try to push it away where we don't have to think about it anymore. Even when Jesus confronts the demons and drives them away, the people of Gerasene still don't want to acknowledge that demons were in their midst. Notice what they do after the demons have been driven off and the possessed man healed:

> And they came to Jesus, and saw the demoniac sitting there, clothed and in his right mind, the man who had had the legion; and they were afraid. And those who had seen it told what had happened to the demoniac and to the swine. And they began to beg Jesus to depart from their neighborhood (Mark 5:15–17).

To accept Jesus into their midst would force them to acknowledge that dark spiritual forces exist. Better to pretend that such evil forces are fairy tales. But if we want to bring about the conversion of souls, changing their eternal destination, then we need to recognize the demonic forces arrayed against us, and beg Jesus to drive them from our midst.

Example

St. Leonard of Port Maurice

St. Leonard of Port Maurice was an Italian Franciscan who lived in the early half of the eighteenth century. He was one of the great preachers of his time, and through his missions (he spent more than forty years preaching!) he brought thousands of people to a fervent practice of the Catholic faith. St. Alphonsus Liguori called him "the great missionary of the eighteenth century." Leonard preached the good news to countless people, and he wasn't afraid to also give his listeners the "bad news." His most famous sermon is entitled "The Little Number of Those Who Are Saved." Its central thesis is, in Leonard's words, "to decide whether the number of Christians who are saved is greater or less than the number of Christians who are damned." The sermon makes for uncomfortable reading for us today, but this canonized saint's methods met with great success. Some excerpts from the sermon:

> It is not vain curiosity but salutary precaution to proclaim from the height of the pulpit certain truths which serve wonderfully to contain the indolence of libertines, who are always talking about the mercy of God and about how easy it is to convert, who live plunged in all sorts of sins and are soundly sleeping on the road to hell. . . .

Poor souls! How can you run so hastily toward hell? For mercy's sake, stop and listen to me for a moment! Either you understand what it means to be saved and to be damned for all eternity, or you do not. If you understand and, in spite of that, you do not decide to change your life today, make a good confession and trample upon the world, in a word, make your every effort to be counted among the littler number of those who are saved, I say that you do not have the Faith. You are more excusable if you do not understand it, for then one must say that you are out of your mind. To be saved for all eternity, to be damned for all eternity, and to not make your every effort to avoid the one and make sure of the other, is something inconceivable. . . .

Cast yourself at the feet of Jesus Christ and say to him, with tearful eyes and contrite heart: "Lord, I confess that up till now I have not lived as a Christian. I am not worthy to be numbered among Your elect. I recognize that I deserve to be damned; but Your mercy is great and, full of confidence in Your grace, I say to You that I want to save my soul, even if I have to sacrifice my fortune, my honor, my very life, as long as I am saved. If I have been unfaithful up to now, I repent, I deplore, I detest my infidelity, I ask You humbly to forgive me for it. Forgive me, good Jesus, and strengthen me also, that I may be saved. I ask You not for wealth, honor or prosperity; I ask you for one thing only, to save my soul."

Leonard recognized the forces arrayed against him in the battle for souls. We should ask for his intercession that we might have the strength to recognize— and to fight—the spiritual enemies who oppose us.

Examination

- Do I believe in hell, *really* believe in it? Do I believe that I or my loved ones could actually go there?

- When evangelizing, do I recognize, in the words of St. Paul, that "we are not contending against flesh and blood, but against the principalities, against the powers, against the world rulers of this present darkness, against the spiritual hosts of wickedness in the heavenly places" (Eph. 6:12)?

Exploration

- Have you ever had any direct encounter with demonic forces?

- How does proclaiming the reality of hell help lead people to heaven?

- Why do most Catholics today avoid talking about the devil?

Exercise

- Read the Gospel of Mark. Note each time Satan or hell is mentioned, and study Christ's attitude toward them.

- Learn the Prayer to St. Michael. Say it every day for the salvation of souls.

- Read Ephesians 6:10–20. Meditate on how Paul's words apply to your work of evangelization.

7

Jesus Refuses
to Tolerate Sin

If the devil and his demons are our enemy, then sin is their greatest weapon. It is through sin that people are lost for Christ, and sin keeps people away from him. So we need to confront sin directly—both in our own life and in the lives of others. But confronting sin in others is often denounced as intolerance, which, ironically, is considered our culture's greatest "sin."

We are required to accept any lifestyle, any choice, and any depravity, all in the name of "tolerance." This poses a problem when it comes to evangelization, for conversion involves rejecting certain lifestyles and choices; in other words, it involves being intolerant of sin.

Encounter

*The encounter with the Samaritan woman
at the well (John 4:1–26)*

[1]Now when the Lord knew that the Pharisees had heard that Jesus was making and baptizing more disciples than John [2](although Jesus himself did not baptize, but only his disciples), [3]he left Judea and departed again to Galilee. [4]He had to pass through Samaria. [5]So he came to a city of Samaria, called Sychar, near the

field that Jacob gave to his son Joseph. [6]Jacob's well was there, and so Jesus, wearied as he was with his journey, sat down beside the well. It was about the sixth hour.

[7]There came a woman of Samaria to draw water. Jesus said to her, "Give me a drink." [8]For his disciples had gone away into the city to buy food. [9]The Samaritan woman said to him, "How is it that you, a Jew, ask a drink of me, a woman of Samaria?" For Jews have no dealings with Samaritans. [10]Jesus answered her, "If you knew the gift of God, and who it is that is saying to you, 'Give me a drink,' you would have asked him, and he would have given you living water." [11]The woman said to him, "Sir, you have nothing to draw with, and the well is deep; where do you get that living water? [12]Are you greater than our father Jacob, who gave us the well, and drank from it himself, and his sons, and his cattle?"

[13]Jesus said to her, "Every one who drinks of this water will thirst again, [14]but whoever drinks of the water that I shall give him will never thirst; the water that I shall give him will become in him a spring of water welling up to eternal life." [15]The woman said to him, "Sir, give me this water, that I may not thirst, nor come here to draw." [16]Jesus said to her, "Go, call your husband, and come here." [17]The woman answered him, "I have no husband." Jesus said to her, "You are right in saying, 'I have no husband'; [18]for you have had five husbands, and he whom you now have is not your husband; this you said truly." [19]The woman said to him, "Sir, I perceive that you are a prophet. [20]Our fathers worshiped on this mountain; and you say that in Jerusalem is the place where men ought to worship." [21]Jesus said to her, "Woman, believe me, the hour is coming when neither on this mountain nor in Jerusalem will

you worship the Father. [22]You worship what you do not know; we worship what we know, for salvation is from the Jews. [23]But the hour is coming, and now is, when the true worshipers will worship the Father in spirit and truth, for such the Father seeks to worship him. [24]God is spirit, and those who worship him must worship in spirit and truth." [25]The woman said to him, "I know that Messiah is coming (he who is called Christ); when he comes, he will show us all things." [26]Jesus said to her, "I who speak to you am he."

Being a Friend

When I started middle school there was a kid, Leo, who really wanted to be my friend. Leo was a good kid, but a bit odd, so he didn't have many friends. For some reason he was convinced that it would be great to be *my* friend. Leo would do all he could to ingratiate himself with me, which, to my shame, led me to push him away. After all, I didn't want to be known as a friend of an "uncool" kid. Yet throughout middle school and into high school he continued to try to be my friend, and all the while I kept him at a distance. I was polite to him, but I made sure we never got close enough for us to be seen as friends. I had a reputation to consider!

At the beginning of our senior year, Leo, who was a very good student, started having issues: his grades declined and he was frequently late for school. One day my dad took me aside and, without revealing any details, told me that things were not good in Leo's household—they never had been, according to my dad—and that I should be nice to him. I took Dad's advice and stopped keeping my distance from Leo. What I discovered was that he was a great guy, and someone who made a great friend. We quickly became close pals, and I regretted my attitude of the previous five years.

Although we went our separate ways after high school, Leo and I stayed in touch (as well as we could in those pre-social media days). A few years after college, Leo started down a bad path and eventually landed in serious legal trouble. I reached out to him and offered any support I could. As we began to reconnect, he revealed to me in more detail his upbringing—it was far more troubled than I ever suspected. His father left his family when Leo was very young, and his mother had a revolving door of boyfriends. She resented having to raise Leo and did little to support him academically, socially, or emotionally. The fact that Leo was simply a bit "odd" and not a full-blown head case was frankly a miracle! I could not imagine being raised as he had been, and my sympathy for him was immense.

He also revealed something else to me, something I never suspected: that he was gay. But having learned just how bad his upbringing had been, I wasn't surprised. He had no real father figure growing up and struggled for years to connect to other boys. Many studies have shown that for certain personalities such an upbringing can result in homosexual tendencies.

Leo knew that I had become a practicing Catholic, and I believe he feared my reaction to the revelation of his homosexuality. His father, after leaving his mother, became a born-again Christian. Although he made no effort to reconcile with Leo's mother (he in fact remarried), he would periodically connect with Leo and involve him in various fundamentalist Christian activities. Leo discovered that most of the people in these groups believed homosexuality to be a choice and that one could simply "pray it away" if he so desired. So Leo assumed that all serious Christians would consider him a sinner who deserved condemnation.

I make no claims to being a particularly compassionate or understanding man. But Leo had been my close friend for years, and I was moved by all he had endured growing up, and by his struggles of the moment. We had long talks about his homosexuality, and I made it clear that I didn't think he had "chosen" his sexual orientation as one might choose a certain flavor of ice cream. I knew that there are significant psychological factors that contribute to the development of homosexual tendencies, and that Leo's upbringing must have had that kind of effect on him. I can't imagine how I would have turned out had I been in his shoes—most likely I'd be a sociopath.

As we talked of ways for him to put his life on a new and better footing, I became nervous. I knew that if I wanted to be a true friend, I would have to advise him to live a chaste life, rejecting the homosexual lifestyle. But if I did so, would he see me as just another judgmental Christian? Would that end our friendship? And if it did, how could I help steer him to a better lifestyle? Since that time I've heard countless similar stories from other Catholics: they have loved ones who have sinful lifestyles—fornication, homosexuality, drug abuse—and they want to confront them about their sins, but (as discussed in chapter 4), they're terrified that speaking up will "end the relationship." Would confronting their loved ones lead them to embrace their sinful lifestyle even more passionately?

Such thoughts have crossed my own mind many times. But even back then I knew that Leo could find peace and solace in his troubled life only by following the teachings of Christ and his Church. If I ignored aspects of his life that kept him mired in sin, our friendship would have a faulty foundation. How could it ever lead him to a true relationship with Christ? So one day I told him, "Leo, I think you need to leave the homosexual lifestyle. It's destructive. It will never bring you true love and happiness. I know you might always have homosexual attractions, but I think the best life for you is to live chastely. You are looking for peace. You can find that only in Christ." The pause that followed seemed to last an eternity.

Happily, Leo listened to me and understood that my advice came out of love, not hatred. After all, we had been close friends for a long time, and he knew that I truly cared about him. My fear of rejection, it turned out, was unfounded: I learned it was possible to confront someone in his sin while still remaining friends.

We often fear that confronting someone about his sins will seem "un-Christian." Yet Christ shows that it is not, as we see from his encounter with the Samaritan woman at the well.

You Have No Husband

Jesus and his disciples are passing through Samaria, whose inhabitants have a strained relationship with the Jews. They decide to take a break in the city of Sychar. As the disciples go off to refresh their supplies, Jesus rests next to Jacob's well. A woman approaches the well, and Jesus asks her for a drink of water. As is typical for the Lord, he uses this ordinary sort of exchange as an opportunity to dive into deeper, spiritual realities. This tactic is itself a model for those who want to evangelize. We all have basic physical needs that everyone recognizes: we get thirsty, we get hungry, we need shelter, and so forth. But most people don't recognize their great *spiritual* needs. So Jesus takes a physical need as an opportunity to launch into a more important discussion about spiritual needs:

> Jesus said to her, "Every one who drinks of this water will thirst again, but whoever drinks of the water that I shall give him will never thirst; the water that I shall give him will become in him a spring of water welling up to eternal life." The woman said to him, "Sir, give me this water, that I may not thirst, nor come here to draw" (John 4:13–15).

Starting with a simple request for a drink, Jesus leads the woman to ask for something herself, something far better: the water that leads to eternal life. She might not yet fully understand Christ's words, but her interest is piqued. Likewise, within our own circle of influence we shouldn't browbeat people with theology, but rather use our ordinary interactions with them to lead them to ask us about eternal matters.

What is especially interesting for our purposes, however, is the response Jesus gives right when he has the Samaritan woman on the cusp of discipleship. Before we look at that, think of how most of us would respond to someone looking for spiritual answers. We would bend over backward to welcome him, and do all we can to answer his questions in a way that satisfies his curiosity but without giving offense. In short, we would strive to do nothing that might turn the inquirer away.

But what does Jesus say to the inquiring Samaritan woman? "Go, call your husband, and come here" (John 4:16). At first glance, it may appear that Jesus wants to include the woman's whole household in this path to salvation. But we find this was not his purpose. The woman answers, "I have no husband," and Jesus responds, "You are right in saying, 'I have no husband'; for you have had five husbands, and he whom you now have is not your husband; this you said truly" (John 4:17–18).

Picture this same scenario playing out at the local parish— a priest bluntly bringing up a woman's marriage history and then noting the irregular status of her current relationship! In all likelihood a letter would be on the bishop's desk within a day or two, and that priest summoned to the chancery for a sharp rebuke and perhaps some "re-education." Yet that priest would be following the example of Jesus, who sees how the Samaritan woman's immoral life stands in the way of her conversion, and so confronts it head-on. Our Lord obviously knew that such a confrontation might lead her to reject him, but his thirst for her salvation compelled him to challenge her lifestyle.

The early Church Fathers called Christ the "Divine Physician." Clement of Alexandria, a second-century Christian, wrote:

The good Instructor, the Wisdom, the Word of the Father, who made man, cares for the whole nature of his creature; the all-sufficient Physician of humanity, the Savior, heals both body and soul. "Rise up," he said to the paralytic; "take the bed on which you lie, and go away home;" and straightway the infirm man received strength. And to the dead he said, "Lazarus, go forth;" and the dead man issued from his coffin such as he was before he died, having undergone resurrection. Further, he heals the soul itself by precepts and gifts—by precepts indeed, in course of time, but being liberal in his gifts, he says to us sinners, "Your sins be forgiven you" (*The Instructor*, bk. 1, chap. 2).

What good physician would ignore unhealthy behavior in a patient? Would he turn a blind eye to a diabetic consuming sugar? Or would he make clear that such behavior is destructive and leads to death? Likewise, when Jesus sees someone in sin, he confronts it directly.

Live and Let Die

Notice also that Jesus doesn't over- or under-react to the woman's immoral past. He confronts her regarding her marriage history, but he doesn't launch into full-scale denunciations of it. He simply makes it clear that her lifestyle is not acceptable for one who would follow him. This balanced approach is all too rare today. In most cases, Catholics simply ignore a person's moral failing, fearing to be labeled "judgmental" or "intolerant." But there is the other extreme. Sometimes, in reaction to the failure of Church leaders to speak out on moral issues, orthodox Catholics jump into condemnation mode, lacking charity and understanding toward another's weakness. This is rare today, but we must nevertheless guard against it.

In our evangelization efforts, we too often flee from confrontation. Our reasons are understandable: we don't want to turn someone away. So we avoid certain topics as if they'll give us a rash (when was the last time you heard contraception discussed at your parish?). This hesitancy is particularly acute among American Catholics. We are, frankly, horrified by the idea of pointing out another person's faults. In a land where "Don't judge me!" has become a mantra, we strive for a "live and let live" attitude toward all. This is, of course, legitimate in most cases. After all, if you're attending your son's Little League practice, you don't turn to the parent sitting next to you and point out the spiritual dangers of adultery.

But if you're guiding someone to a deeper knowledge and practice of the Catholic faith, his or her moral life must become a topic at some point. In the politically incorrect words of St. Paul, "Do you not know that the unrighteous will not inherit the kingdom of God? Do not be deceived; neither the immoral, nor idolaters, nor adulterers, nor homosexuals, nor thieves, nor the greedy, nor drunkards, nor revilers, nor robbers will inherit the kingdom of God" (1 Cor. 6:9–10). If someone is living a life contrary to the gospel, he has erected a barrier to God that must be torn down, and as an evangelizer, you need to hand him the tools to begin the process. Gently and lovingly, you must help him confront and correct any lifestyle choices that block him from receiving God's graces.

Of course, the same standard applies to us as well. If we do not acknowledge our own sins and bring them to confession, then we can't confront others. This doesn't mean we have to be perfect, but it does mean that we must recognize our faults and work to overcome them.

My friend Leo is still an active homosexual, many years after I first confronted him about his lifestyle. He and I have remained friends, and he knows my views on homosexual activity. I haven't brought it up to him in years, but I've been careful not to say or do anything to contradict the Church's teachings. Confronting someone's sins might lead to his immediate repentance—let's call that the "Nineveh response"—or it might lead to repentance years or decades later—the "St. Augustine response"—or it might lead to no change in behavior—the "Sodom and Gomorrah response." The response, however, is not our responsibility; we simply have a duty to show the way to eternal life. It's up to each individual—my friend Leo or the Samaritan woman or your friend in a sinful lifestyle—to make the decisions necessary to take that path.

Example

St. Pio of Pietrelcina (Padre Pio)

St. Pio of Pietrelcina, better known as Padre Pio, was a Capuchin friar of the twentieth century who was world-renowned for his holiness. He received the stigmata at the age of twenty-eight and bore them until his death at the age of eighty-one. Padre Pio is one of the most popular saints of our day, with countless avid devotees.

Padre Pio spent much of his ministry in the confessional, and he was known to have supernatural insight into people's souls. Penitents came from all over the world to have him hear their confessions; he heard hundreds of thousands of them in his lifetime. This was in spite (or perhaps because) of the fact that he was quite blunt when confronting people's sins. He never minced words and always demanded true contrition before giving absolution. A few examples include:

A man told Padre Pio: "Father, I tell lies when I am with some friends of mine. I do it in order to make everybody happy." Padre Pio responded: "Oh, do you want to go to hell by joking?!"

A doctor was in confession with Padre Pio. He confessed his sins and waited for absolution. Padre Pio asked him if he had other things to add, but the doctor replied that he did not. Then Padre Pio reminded him, "Keep in mind that on holy days you cannot miss Mass, because this is a mortal sin." The doctor remembered he had missed Sunday Mass a few months before and immediately confessed this.

A woman told Padre Pio that she was worried about her aunt who read Tarot cards. Padre Pio in a commanding voice said: "Throw that stuff away, as soon as you can."

A few quotes from Padre Pio that further exemplify his hatred of sin and his willingness to confront it:

"Divorce is the passport to hell."

"The day in which people . . . lose the horror of the abortion, it will be the most terrible day for humanity."

"If you have the courage to imitate Mary Magdalene in her sins, have the courage to imitate her penance!"

More important than anything for Padre Pio was the salvation of souls. He was willing to make people uncomfortable, and to endure rejection, in order to bring people closer to Christ. He can be our model when we hesitate to confront sin in ourselves and others.

Examination

- Am I willing to overcome a fear of being labeled "judgmental?"

- Do I believe that sins are barriers to true conversion—and believe it enough to confront them?

Exploration

- Why do you think our culture has exalted "tolerance" as the greatest virtue?

- What are some actions and attitudes that our culture *doesn't* tolerate?

- What sin is most often ignored or tolerated by Catholics today?

Exercise

- Read 1 Corinthians. Explore the different ways St. Paul confronted the sins of the Corinthian church.

- Reflect on your own life. What sins do you tolerate or excuse in yourself, but condemn when you see them in others?

- Is there a moral teaching that is difficult for you to proclaim? Resolve to learn more about the wisdom of that teaching through studying Scripture, the *Catechism*, and other solid sources.

8

Jesus Doesn't Water Down
His Teachings

In every day and age there are particular teachings of the Church that go against the grain; the Catholic faith is always countercultural. And Jesus warned that following him would not be easy: "If any man would come after me, let him deny himself and take up his cross and follow me" (Matt. 16:24). Today the Church teachings that are most often rejected are those having to do with sexual morality and the sanctity of all human life from conception to natural death.

Sometimes we want to water down those "hard teachings" in order to attract people to the Church. But this was not Christ's method, and to be like him we must charitably and clearly proclaim his "hard teachings" even when they conflict with our culture.

Encounter

The dispute with the Pharisees regarding divorce (Matt. 19:3–9)

[3]And Pharisees came up to him and tested him by asking, "Is it lawful to divorce one's wife for any cause?" [4]He answered, "Have you not read that he who made them from the beginning made them male and female, [5]and said, 'For this reason a man shall leave his father and mother and be joined to his wife, and the two

shall become one'? [6]So they are no longer two but one. What therefore God has joined together, let not man put asunder." [7]They said to him, "Why then did Moses command one to give a certificate of divorce, and to put her away?" [8]He said to them, "For your hardness of heart Moses allowed you to divorce your wives, but from the beginning it was not so. [9]And I say to you: whoever divorces his wife, except for unchastity, and marries another, commits adultery; and he who marries a divorced woman, commits adultery."

I'm Sorry

One day I was meeting with a pastor and some of his staff about launching evangelization efforts in their parish. The pastor had a sincere longing to bring people back to the Church, and he lamented the large numbers who had abandoned the Faith in recent decades. But during our discussion he repeatedly blamed the Church itself for this mass exodus, insisting that evangelization should consist primarily of apologizing to disaffected Catholics.

At first I assumed he meant apologizing for the clergy sex-abuse scandals, and naturally I agreed with him about that. After all, I knew that even lesser wrongs committed by priests can drive people away from the Church. I once met a woman who married before she was twenty, due to pressure from her mother, and whose husband made it clear before they were married that he had no desire to have children. Unsurprisingly, the marriage lasted less than a year. After her divorce, her parish priest told her that she was no longer welcome to receive Communion— a statement at odds with the Church's practice, which allows Catholics who are divorced but not remarried to receive. So she left the Church and began attending an Episcopal church, where she ended up marrying the pastor's son. I met her twenty years later, when she attended an "Ask Any Question" meeting wanting to know if it was possible to return to the Catholic Church. Think of it: this poor woman had been away for over twenty years because of the harsh words of a single priest! I put her in touch with our pastor to discuss getting an annulment (I'm not a canon lawyer, but the case for the invalidity of her first marriage seemed pretty airtight).

So, to return to my meeting with the pastor who wanted to start an evangelization campaign: only after some further discussion did I realize that he wanted to apologize not only for the sins of Church leaders but for some of the Church's *teachings*, particularly the most countercultural ones, such as those prohibiting contraception, abortion, and divorce.

Hardness of Heart

Unfortunately, this pastor's attitude is widespread among Catholics—both lay and clerical—far too many of whom downplay or even deny certain Church teachings to keep the pews full; they want to lighten what they see as an impossible burden.

Things were similar in Christ's day. Although in our day the word Pharisee is used to characterize a harsh "rightwinger," the Pharisees of Christ's time in fact advocated relaxed laws regarding divorce and remarriage. In Matthew 19 we see them challenge Jesus on this issue, looking for ways to trip him up. According to the law of Moses, it was permissible for a man to divorce his wife (Deut. 24:1–4). But Jesus supersedes this law, harkening back to the time of Creation: "Have you not read that he who made them from the beginning made them male and female, and said, 'For this reason a man shall leave his father and mother and be joined to his wife, and the two shall become one'? So they are no longer two but one. What therefore God has joined together, let not man put asunder" (Matt. 19:4–6). As for Moses' permission for divorce, he explains: "For your hardness of heart Moses allowed you to divorce your wives, but from the beginning it was not so. And I say to you: whoever divorces his wife, except for unchastity, and marries another, commits adultery; and he who marries a divorced woman, commits adultery" (Matt. 19:8–9).

It's important to remember that when the Pharisees challenged Christ, they did so as publicly as possible, hoping to discredit him. So when they asked him about divorce, they likely did so in front of a crowd, including Jews who were themselves divorced. Yet Christ didn't hesitate to uphold the stricter law of marriage, and made it clear that to remarry after a divorce is "adultery" (Matt. 19:9). Such a "hard teaching" was surely difficult for some in the crowd to hear, and no doubt Jesus lost followers by insisting on it.

So, just as Jesus didn't soften his teachings about divorce and remarriage in his own time, neither should we in ours. We have already seen how the modern acceptance of divorce has led to widespread suffering, especially on the part of women and children. So, while obeying the "hard teachings" of Jesus may sometimes be painful, obeying them is necessary to prevent even greater pain.

Enthusiasm Attracts

The logic behind avoiding the "hard teachings" while evangelizing is simple:

- We want to evangelize and bring people into the Church.
- The "hard teachings" will drive people away from the Church.
- Therefore, we must minimize, ignore, or even reject these "hard teachings."

On the surface this logic is impeccable. In reality it leads to the Episcopal Church. No denomination has done more to soften its teachings and make itself socially acceptable than the Episcopalians. How did that work out for them? According to the *Episcopal Church Annual*, in 1965 there were 3,615,000 baptized Episcopalians. Every year following showed a decline, and by 2014, there were only 1,956,042 baptized members, a 46 percent decrease. The conclusion is inescapable: making its teachings more attractive led to a mass exodus.

Perhaps counterintuitively, then, the result of avoiding Christ's "hard teachings" isn't flocks of people coming through the church doors, but the opposite. After all, why would someone make the sacrifice of getting up early on Sunday and spending an hour sitting in a pew to hear a message they could hear 24/7 from the mainstream media? If a church says—either explicitly or implicitly—that the vows of marriage can be broken, what distinguishes that church from everyone else? Why bother listening to it?

This does not mean that proclaiming the "hard teachings" boldly will result in a massive number of conversions and full pews. After all, they're called "hard teachings" because they are *hard*. Many people will find them *too* hard and reject them, and reject the messenger who preaches them.

But what is the goal of evangelization? Just to have full pews? No, the real goal is *making disciples*. In his final words to his apostles, Christ said, "Go therefore and make disciples of all nations, baptizing them in the name of the Father and of the Son and of the Holy Spirit, teaching them to observe all that I have commanded you" (Matt. 28:19–20). Note these words carefully, for they are the marching orders of every Catholic evangelist:

1. "Make disciples." We're not trying to get people to join a club; we're inviting them to make a radical commitment that will change their lives dramatically. This makes evangelization fundamentally different from any membership drive or marketing program.

2. "Baptizing them." Becoming a disciple means entering the Church and living a sacramental life, which entails certain prohibitions. For example, one cannot receive any other sacraments until one is baptized, cannot receive Communion if not in a state of grace, and cannot get married if there are any impediments to marriage. To live a sacramental life, then, requires abiding by some strict rules.

3. "Teaching them to observe all that I have commanded you." Note that Jesus said "all." *None* of Christ's teachings are superfluous; in no instance do we find him allowing his disciples to pick and choose which teachings they will follow. He knows that we will find our true fulfillment only if we submit to all he asks of us.

Is the goal of our parish's RCIA classes to bring about real conversions, even if only a few, or simply to fill the seats? If the latter, we will be sorely tempted to reshape the gospel in a way we believe will attract the most numbers, though as we have noted that doesn't work. Jesus himself focused on a relatively small number of disciples, challenging them constantly and never softening his teachings in order to make them feel more comfortable. As a result, they would eventually transform the world.

I once helped out with a well-established parish RCIA program, and I remember vividly the first class I attended. We met in the church basement, with about a dozen or so catechumens in attendance. They were of varied backgrounds: a few were devoted Protestants who had already become convinced of the truth of Catholicism; some had been dragged there by Catholic spouses (usually husbands by their wives); others were fallen-away Catholics who were considering returning to the practice of the Faith; and some were there by invitation from a friend.

Once everyone was introduced, the RCIA leader made it clear what direction the classes would take: they would teach the basics of Catholic doctrine—and apologize for the basics of Catholic morality. Since there is little controversy today regarding the Trinity, he felt no need to tone that teaching down. But on controversial topics such as contraception, he took a more laissez-faire attitude: you could believe those teachings if you want, but no one would object if you rejected them. He never claimed that any particular teachings of the Church were false; in fact, if asked his opinion on them he would say things like "I am a faithful son of the Church." Which is like a son saying about his mother, "Look, guys, I know my mom's off her rocker, but she's my mom, so I'm gonna stick with her." In other words, the Church's teachings are not to be embraced but apologized for.

Contrast that attitude with that of a young couple I once recruited to teach marriage preparation classes, Rob and Allison. They were in their late twenties and had three kids. They were on fire for their faith and loved telling others about it. The marriage prep program we used did not shy away from the Church's "hard teachings" about human sexuality, which this young couple not only lived joyfully themselves but whose wisdom they were eager to communicate to others.

How, exactly, did they do this? One example is how they handled the "untouchable" subject of artificial contraception. Now, over the years I've seen this subject dealt with in a variety of ways, most of them similar to the way to handle an explosive device or a soiled diaper. One marriage prep instructor, for instance, talked about Natural Family Planning (NFP) from a very clinical, distant point of view, and admitted (without explanation) that she and her husband never practiced it. Another instructor rushed through his presentation on NFP as if the building were on fire. But Rob and Allison were neither embarrassed nor apologetic in their discussion of contraception and NFP. They shared their own experience of how NFP had drawn them closer together, while being honest about the challenges involved. They studied the science behind contraception and NFP, so they could answer any questions or objections that might arise. In effect, they were a walking, talking advertisement against using artificial contraception!

We offered marriage preparation classes in parishes throughout the diocese, taught by many couples. After each class, we surveyed the participants for feedback. One standard question concerned the attendee's attitude toward contraception both before and after attending the class. We found that, before attending the class, the vast majority of couples had been planning to use artificial contraception in their marriage. Since our program had a lot of good material promoting NFP, when the classes were over a good number of couples—around 40 percent—said they would now consider NFP instead of artificial contraception. But for the couples who took marriage preparation from Rob and Allison, over 70 percent said afterward they would consider NFP! By treating the "hard teachings" as something to make their lives better—and therefore to be joyfully embraced—Rob and Allison were able to bring others to see their beauty.

This gets to the core of the issue: what Catholicism teaches is far deeper, far more meaningful, and far more joyful than what the world does. Yes, it often demands more of us, but it also bears more and better fruit. By undercutting Church teachings to make them more like the world's, we paradoxically make the Church *less* attractive, not more. When I was first exploring Catholicism, a Catholic friend compared it to a delicious seven-course meal: it has everything to delight the palate and satisfy your hunger. Anything less is a poor substitute—more like fast food. As Catholic evangelists, then, we should always follow Christ's lead and proclaim all of his teachings—even the hard ones—with joy and confidence, knowing they are the path to eternal happiness.

Example

St. Teresa of Calcutta

St. Teresa of Calcutta (popularly known as Mother Teresa) was one of the most famous people of the late twentieth century. Which is surprising, for she wasn't a glamorous movie star, well-known athlete, or powerful politician. She was just a simple nun who cared for the "poorest of the poor" in the name of Christ in the worst areas of world.

Many famous people avoid controversy so as not to lose admirers. Not St. Teresa. When it came to Catholic teaching, she took controversy by the horns.

In 1994, for instance, she was invited to speak at the National Prayer Breakfast in Washington, DC. This annual event is typically non-controversial—an opportunity for politicians to appear receptive to people of faith. But St. Teresa saw it as an opportunity to tell those politicians—including then-President Bill Clinton and his wife, Hillary, both in attendance and both vehemently pro-abortion—an important truth that many of them did not want to hear:

> But I feel that the greatest destroyer of peace today is abortion, because it is a war against the child, a direct killing of the innocent child, murder by the mother herself. And if we accept that a mother can kill even her own child, how can we tell other people not to kill one another? How do we persuade a woman not to have an abortion? As always, we must persuade her with love and we remind ourselves that love means to be willing to give until it hurts. Jesus gave even his life to love us. So, the mother who is thinking of abortion, should be helped to love, that is, to give until it hurts her plans, or her free time, to respect the life of her child. The father of that child, whoever he is, must also give until it hurts.
>
> By abortion, the mother does not learn to love, but kills even her own child to solve her problems. And, by abortion, the father is told that he does not have to take any responsibility at all for the child he has brought into the world. That father is likely to put other women into the same trouble. So abortion just leads to more abortion. Any country that accepts abortion is not teaching its people to love, but to

use any violence to get what they want. This is why the greatest destroyer of love and peace is abortion.

Mother Teresa didn't care who she might offend; she cared only to defend Christ's teachings about the sanctity of all human life, born and unborn. We may never be called to proclaim the "hard teachings" to the rich and powerful, but sometimes it takes just as much courage to do so in our own modest spheres of influence.

Examination

- Am I afraid that certain moral teachings of the Church turn people away? Do I soften those teachings in order to attract others?

- Do I see these hard teachings as a burden, or do I joyfully proclaim them as a path to happiness with Christ?

Exploration

- Why does trying to make Church teachings more palatable actually make them less beautiful?

- Why do you think God allowed divorce in the time of Moses, but restored its ban under Christ?

- What do you think is the Church's "hardest" teaching today?

Exercise

- Read *Evangelium Vitae* by Pope St. John Paul II.

- Find out when the next 40 Days for Life is happening in your area, and join in praying for mothers and children in front of an abortion clinic.

- If you are not familiar with Natural Family Planning, research it (one place to start is the Couple to Couple League), and learn why it is consistent with Church teaching.

Being a
Truly Catholic
Evangelist

9

Jesus Proclaims
the Fullness of the Faith

Evangelical Protestants have a reputation for being good evangelists—that's why they're called "Evangelicals," right? On the other hand, modern Catholics have a reputation for being *terrible* at evangelization. So we look to Protestant evangelists like Billy Graham, or even "Prosperity Gospel" preachers like Joel Osteen, and try to emulate them. And no doubt they are worthy of emulation in some respects. But we must always remember that we are *Catholic* evangelists, and the "Catholic" part isn't an add-on. It's essential to our message. We can't downplay teachings such as the Real Presence of Christ in the Eucharist, or our veneration of the Blessed Virgin Mary. We can't assume that by preaching difficult or controversial doctrines we will turn others off and "lose" potential converts.

Christ's teachings form an indivisible whole. In charity, we must present the full gospel to others, for it is the full gospel that brings eternal life.

Encounter

The desertion by some disciples over the
Real Presence (John 6:51–66)

[51]"I am the living bread which came down from heaven; if any one eats of this bread, he will live for ever;

and the bread which I shall give for the life of the world is my flesh."

[52]The Jews then disputed among themselves, saying, "How can this man give us his flesh to eat?" [53]So Jesus said to them, "Truly, truly, I say to you, unless you eat the flesh of the Son of man and drink his blood, you have no life in you; [54]he who eats my flesh and drinks my blood has eternal life, and I will raise him up at the last day. [55]For my flesh is food indeed, and my blood is drink indeed. [56]He who eats my flesh and drinks my blood abides in me, and I in him. [57]As the living Father sent me, and I live because of the Father, so he who eats me will live because of me. [58]This is the bread which came down from heaven, not such as the fathers ate and died; he who eats this bread will live for ever." [59]This he said in the synagogue, as he taught at Capernaum.

[60]Many of his disciples, when they heard it, said, "This is a hard saying; who can listen to it?" [61]But Jesus, knowing in himself that his disciples murmured at it, said to them, "Do you take offense at this? [62]Then what if you were to see the Son of man ascending where he was before? [63]It is the spirit that gives life, the flesh is of no avail; the words that I have spoken to you are spirit and life. [64]But there are some of you that do not believe." For Jesus knew from the first who those were that did not believe, and who it was that would betray him. [65]And he said, "This is why I told you that no one can come to me unless it is granted him by the Father." [66]After this many of his disciples drew back and no longer went about with him.

Building the Foundation

Why did God make you?

Ask this question of Catholics of a certain age, and they'll immediately respond: "God made me to know him, to love him, and to serve him in this world, and to be happy with him forever in the next."

This is one of the most memorable questions in the *Baltimore Catechism*, the text that generations of Catholics in this country were raised on. Set up in question-and-answer format, it was drilled into Catholic children, who were required to memorize large portions of it. In the 1970s, however, this method of catechesis fell out of favor, and soon the *Baltimore Catechism* was replaced by a legion of competing texts, all promising to help young Catholics *really* know their faith. It became common to mock the religious instruction of previous generations, claiming with a superior air, "Rote answers aren't enough—they need to understand the *why* of their faith!" True as far as it goes, but that doesn't mean that integrating doctrine into the fabric of your being at a young age isn't a strong foundation for a life of Catholic discipleship.

My father-in-law was one of those millions raised on the *Baltimore Catechism*. He remained faithful to the Church throughout his life, even though he didn't approve of some of the changes made in the Church in the 1960s and '70s, particularly the changes to the Mass. Once my wife asked him, "Why didn't you lose your faith or leave the Church— as so many did—when those changes happened?" My father-in-law—a simple man (and I say that as a supreme compliment)—replied, "Because Christ promised that the gates of hell would not prevail against the Church." It was like an answer out of the *Baltimore Catechism*, yet it was not a rote answer he was giving. Yes, the doctrine of the indefectibility of the Church had been drilled into him as a boy, but he had made that doctrine his own. When everything in the Church seemed to be crumbling (and I think younger Catholics underestimate how disorienting those changes were to Catholics of the time), he clung to this doctrine, a lifeline in those turbulent waters. Doctrine gave him the foundation to resist despair.

Now compare that with the experiences of Catholics raised in the 1970s, after the *Baltimore Catechism* had been ejected from the curriculum. A priest friend of mine, who grew up back then, once told me that he learned two things in the catechism classes of his youth: "Be nice and don't do drugs." That's it. Fortunately for him, he had a family environment that fostered his faith and kept him in the Church, but most of his classmates fled the Church almost as soon as they finished high school. They couldn't leave quickly enough. As soon as they encountered temptations to leave the Faith, they had no foundation to resist them. They didn't even know about the gates of hell—they were too busy running through them.

Do You Take Offense at This?

People fleeing the Church because of difficulties with doctrine is nothing new. During the sixteenth century, whole swaths of the European population left the Catholic Church, embracing simple slogans such as "Scripture alone" and "faith alone." Charismatic heretics such as Martin Luther offered the faithful a sweeter-sounding, though false, presentation of the gospel. Yet the Catholic Church did not change its teachings even in the face of mass apostasy, knowing that it must remain true to the totality of Christ's teachings.

Jesus himself knew what it was like to be abandoned by his followers, as we see in his famous Bread of Life discourse (John 6). Foretelling his gift of the sacrament of the Eucharist, he says, "I am the bread of life" (John 6:35) and "if any one eats of this bread, he will live for ever; and the bread which I give for the life of the world is my flesh" (John 6:51). Saints, mystics, and ordinary laypeople have meditated on these words for two thousand years, recognizing the Real Presence of the Lord in the Eucharist. But from the moment they were spoken, and down through the ages, they have been among the most difficult words for potential disciples of Christ to accept: "the Jews then disputed among themselves, saying, 'How can this man give us his flesh to eat?'" (John 6:52). (If we put ourselves in their shoes, we will sympathize with their perplexity. After all, how would we respond to a preacher saying we must eat his flesh to have eternal life?) Jesus then doubles down on his teaching, telling his listeners that "unless you eat the flesh of the Son of man and drink his blood, you have no life in you" (John 6:53). To a Jew, the idea of drinking blood—any blood—was abhorrent. Even Christ's disciples challenge him on this teaching: "This is a hard saying, who can listen to it?" (John 6:60).

How does Jesus respond? Does he backpedal to make his teaching more palatable? No, he simply challenges them to accept it on his word. As a result, "many of his disciples drew back and no longer went about with him" (John 6:66). These are people who clearly have some desire to follow Christ, yet they reject his explicit teachings—his doctrine—about the Real Presence. They were the forerunners of today's "spiritual but not religious" movement! Jesus allowed them to leave. Refusing to accept his teachings—his doctrines—means refusing to be his disciple.

We Are All Religious

What do I mean when I say "spiritual but not religious"? It's a popular saying among those who believe in a spiritual world but also believe that "organized religion"—with its doctrines, rules, and rituals—is unnecessary for a strong spiritual life, perhaps even harmful to it. Needless to say, such people disdain the Catholic Church, and unfortunately, many of them are former Catholics.

Ironically, some of Christ's own words give impetus to this movement, though only through an erroneous interpretation of them. While dining with some Pharisees, Jesus is scolded for omitting the Jewish ritual washings before the meal (Luke 11:38). He in turn harshly criticizes them: "Now you Pharisees cleanse the outside of the cup and of the dish, but inside you are full of extortion and wickedness. You fools! Did not he who made the outside make the inside also?" (Luke 11:39–40). To the "spiritual but not religious" crowd, this is a clear indication that religious activities aren't important—only what's in the heart!

Properly understood, however, what Jesus is condemning in this passage is the belief that external religious observances are *all* that is needed to be a true follower of God. In other words, he warns against having sinful thoughts and dark desires while keeping up outward religious appearances, in an attempt either to satisfy God or to protect one's standing in the community. Nowhere does Jesus condemn religious practices themselves, and in fact he can be seen engaging in them: he attends the synagogue regularly (Mark 3, Luke 13) and participates in the Jewish holy days (John 2:13; 6:4; 11:55). His disciples too, after his ascension and the descent of the Holy Spirit at Pentecost, continue to attend the temple services and take part in Jewish religious practices (Acts 2:46; 3:1). If Jesus had condemned such practices on principle, surely his most devoted followers—guided by the Holy Spirit—would have discontinued them immediately.

Humans are inherently religious. We see this in the flourishing of religions throughout history everywhere in the world. No culture has ever existed that didn't have religion. Even atheistic societies such as Nazi Germany and Soviet Russia had their religion: the State. If you watch any footage of their parades and other spectacles, you can't help but notice how liturgical and religious they are. Man naturally desires to follow a religion. Even those in the "spiritual but not religious" crowd end up following quasi-religious rituals, albeit ones of their own devising. Whether communing with nature at the beach, meditating at home amid candles and incense, or even worshipping at the altar of Sunday afternoon football, everyone is religious.

But what matters is whether the religion one follows is *true*, and whether it leads one to the deeper inner life to which Jesus refers. The religious practices, doctrines, and rituals of Catholicism have their origin in the teaching of Jesus and his apostles, and have been honed for almost two thousand years under the direction of the Holy Spirit. They strengthen the inner spiritual life. The fact is, you can't really be spiritual without being religious, and you can't be an authentic disciple of Jesus without doctrine and ritual.

Unfortunately, in many evangelization circles, we have forgotten Christ's model. We underemphasize doctrine in a misguided effort to attract more people. Over and over in my evangelization work I have heard well-intentioned Catholics water down the Faith, usually with regard to doctrines that stand out as particularly Catholic. In our eagerness to bring people into the Church, we want to make the on-ramp as smooth as possible. The intention might be noble, but it doesn't yield well-formed Catholics.

Catholic, or Catholic Lite?

I mentioned in the introduction that while in college I was involved in Campus Crusade for Christ. This Evangelical "parachurch" pressures its members to share the "Four Spiritual Laws" with non-Christians in order to persuade them to "make a decision for Christ." These Four Spiritual Laws are:

1. God loves you and offers a wonderful plan for your life.
2. Man is sinful and separated from God. Therefore, he cannot know and experience God's love and plan for his life.
3. Jesus Christ is God's only provision for man's sin. Through him you can know and experience God's love and plan for your life.
4. We must individually receive Jesus Christ as Savior and Lord; then we can know and experience God's love and plan for our lives.

As you can see, these "laws" contain some basic Christian truths. As always, however, the devil is in the details. For example, what is meant by "individually receive Jesus Christ as Savior and Lord"? Catholics say that you first "receive Jesus" at baptism, and later continue to receive him sacramentally in the Eucharist. But this is most emphatically *not* what members of Campus Crusade think. They believe that "receiving Jesus" is just a decision that one makes, by which one becomes a Christian. Baptism is not necessary, nor is reception of the Eucharist.

Also, what is *not* said in these Four Spiritual Laws is as important as what *is* said. What about the need for repentance? The importance of living a moral life? Indeed, a whole host of things that make up the Christian life are left unmentioned. True, when presenting the gospel it's important to start with the simple and then work up to more details. But too often we're afraid to get into the details of doctrine and practice at all because we think that those things will turn people away. Instead we focus only on the easiest and simplest aspects of Christianity—the parts about love and acceptance. These are important to the Christian message, but by themselves they are an amputated Christianity.

When it comes to evangelization, many Catholics feel insecure when they compare themselves with Evangelicals, whose very name declares their desire to bring people to Jesus. So we borrow their methodology, thinking we'll just stick the "Catholic stuff" in at the end. This approach is fundamentally flawed. It assumes that Catholicism is merely "Protestantism Plus." But in fact, all that "Catholic stuff"—including doctrines such as the Eucharist and the perpetual virginity of the Mary—is essential to the Christian faith. How, for instance, can one teach about Christ's passion and death without teaching also about our participation in that passion and death during the Mass? Reception of the holy Eucharist is not incidental to the Christian life—it is indispensable: "Truly, truly, I say to you, unless you eat the flesh of the Son of man and drink his blood, you have no life in you" (John 6:53). Doctrine matters.

Catholic doctrine is an integrated whole. What St. Paul said of the body of the Church is also true of its body of teachings: "As it is, there are many parts, yet one body. The eye cannot say to the hand, 'I have no need of you,' nor again the head to the feet, 'I have no need of you.' On the contrary, the parts of the body which seem to be weaker are indispensable, and those parts of the body which we think less honorable we invest with the greater honor, and our unpresentable parts are treated with greater modesty" (1 Cor. 12:20–23). One cannot understand the dignity of the human person without an understanding of the Trinity; nor can one understand the full impact of sin without an understanding of purgatory.

Does that mean that when we are evangelizing a non-Catholic—or a fallen-away Catholic—we should ask him to memorize the *Baltimore Catechism*? Of course not. What is appropriate for a Catholic child is not necessarily appropriate for an adult. What's important is that, like Jesus, we not shy away from teaching even the most "difficult" doctrine.

Many people instinctively recognize the shallowness of the Evangelical notion of the "sinner's prayer." This was the end goal of the Four Spiritual Laws: to have someone recite a specific prayer to receive Jesus as his Lord and Savior, at which point he obtains eternal salvation. Sounds easy, and it is, but most people perceive that there must be more to being a Christian than this. And rightly so. The Catholic teaching on salvation is much richer: we mystically enter into the passion, death, and resurrection of Christ through the sacraments. As St. Paul wrote:

> Do you not know that all of us who have been baptized into Christ Jesus were baptized into his death? We were buried therefore with him by baptism into death, so that as Christ was raised from the dead by the glory of the Father, we too might walk in newness of life (Rom. 6:3–4).

Further, at the Last Supper Christ himself instituted the Eucharist and connected it to his sacrifice on Calvary. Receiving the Eucharist, in a sense, transports us back to Calvary and allows us to participate in those sacred mysteries. The reality of the sacraments and how our participation in them draws us into salvation history is not an "add-on" to the gospel message we share with others—it is essential to it. Here we see the paradox most clearly: what at first seems more complex and difficult in actuality reveals Christ's teachings at their most beautiful. This reality can be likened to stained glass windows: in recent years many such windows have been "simplified," displaying just a few colors in a cartoon-like design. Compared with classic, and detailed, images of events from salvation history depicted in older windows, these newer windows leave the observer wanting more. Likewise, when we try to simplify our Lord's teachings in order to make them more palatable, we actually reduce their attraction.

Evangelization means making disciples, and part of the task of discipleship is trusting our Lord even when we don't understand his teachings. My father-in-law didn't understand why things were changing in the Church, but he trusted in Christ and remained faithful to him even while others were fleeing. In this way he modeled himself on the apostle Peter. After many of the disciples left Jesus due to his teaching on the Eucharist, Christ turned to the Twelve and asked, "Will you also go away?" But Peter answered, "Lord, to whom shall we go? You have the words of eternal life, and we have believed, and have come to know, that you are the Holy One of God" (John 6:67–69). Peter didn't understand any better than those who left how he would eat Christ's flesh and drink his blood. Yet he trusted in Christ, and this made him a true disciple. If we hide or downplay certain doctrinal difficulties when we evangelize, we take away the opportunity for others to trust in the way Peter (and my father-in-law) did. After all, they aren't taking *our* word for it, but are instead taking *Christ's* word for it.

Let's not present a "Catholic Lite" version of the gospel, avoiding anything we think might be too demanding or difficult for our hearers. Nor should we give just the basic

Protestant message, then try to graft on the Catholic parts later; the gospel presented must be Catholic through and through. Instead of short-changing our hearers, let's present to them the complete gospel—with all its doctrines, all its wonder and beauty.

Example

St. Thomas Aquinas

The goal of every Catholic is to be a saint. Thomas Aquinas attained this goal. But he was also something else: one of the most celebrated intellects of all time. He used his incredible mind to explain and defend the doctrines of the Catholic Church. His most famous work is the *Summa Theologica*, a systematic exposition of a host of philosophical and theological subjects. Although unfinished, it is considered a towering achievement and has been a standard text for theologians ever since.

But another of Thomas's works, although less celebrated, deserves attention: the *Summa contra Gentiles*. It was written to assist Catholic missionaries in their work of winning converts. It was intended in particular to aid evangelization of Muslims and Jews. Structured in four "books," it begins with a defense of monotheism, a Catholic teaching with which Muslims and Jews agree. Then it moves on to uniquely Christian doctrines, explaining why they are true and why the contradictory teachings of non-Catholic religions are false.

Thomas understood that evangelization requires a solid foundation in Catholic doctrine. For him, it wasn't a matter of appealing to a lowest common denominator. He applied his great intellect to helping missionaries overcome any obstacles people might have to Catholic doctrine, for true conversion could come only to those who embraced the totality of the teachings of Christ.

Examination

- Do I shy away from proclaiming particularly "Catholic" doctrines?

- Do I present the Faith in a "least common denominator" way, hoping it will less often be rejected?

Exploration

- Why didn't Jesus make more of an effort to bring back the disciples who left him after the Bread of Life discourse in John 6?

- What is missing from the Four Spiritual Laws?

- Do you think memorization is important in religious education? Why or why not?

Exercise

- Start a study of the *Catechism of the Catholic Church*. Resolve to read one section a day during Advent or Lent.

- The Blessed Virgin Mary is a stumbling block to many Protestants. Read *Redemptoris Mater* by Pope St. John Paul II to gain a deeper appreciation of the Blessed Mother.

- Form a debate club with fellow Catholics and Protestant friends. Debate the various doctrines that separate us.

10

Jesus Brings About Repentance

If you're a Protestant involved in evangelization, you want people to pray the "sinner's prayer." But if you're Catholic, you know that's not sufficient, so what do you direct people toward? In most cases, the sacrament of penance. Whether you're talking to a fallen-away Catholic or a baptized Protestant, that person will need to go to confession to be reconciled with Christ and his Church. And not only is confession the entryway for those who wish to live a Catholic life; it's also the weapon that destroys sin. It is the most powerful weapon in a Catholic evangelist's arsenal.

Unfortunately, most of us neglect promoting confession. As Catholic evangelists we must make it integral to our proclamation of Christ's teachings and of what it means to be his disciples.

Encounter

The contrition of Peter after the miraculous catch (Luke 5:1–10)

¹While the people pressed upon him to hear the word of God, he was standing by the lake of Gennesaret. ²And he saw two boats by the lake; but the fishermen had gone out of them and were washing their nets. ³Getting into one of the boats, which was Simon's, he asked him to put out a little from the land. And he sat down and taught the people from the boat. ⁴And

when he had ceased speaking, he said to Simon, "Put out into the deep and let down your nets for a catch." [5]And Simon answered, "Master, we toiled all night and took nothing! But at your word I will let down the nets." [6]And when they had done this, they enclosed a great shoal of fish; and as their nets were breaking, [7]they beckoned to their partners in the other boat to come and help them. And they came and filled both the boats, so that they began to sink. [8]But when Simon Peter saw it, he fell down at Jesus' knees, saying, "Depart from me, for I am a sinful man, O Lord." [9]For he was astonished, and all that were with him, at the catch of fish which they had taken; [10]and so also were James and John, sons of Zebedee, who were partners with Simon. And Jesus said to Simon, "Do not be afraid; henceforth you will be catching men."

Are You Listening, God?

During my sophomore year in high school I had a conversion experience. I was a member of my Methodist church's youth group, and one spring weekend we traveled to an out-of-state Christian college for a youth retreat. At an evening session, while Michael W. Smith's "Friends" was playing in the background, one of the speakers made an "altar call." Well, it was in an auditorium, so it was more of a "stage call," I guess. At any rate, I responded. I asked Jesus to become my personal Lord and Savior and invited him into my heart.

Needless to say, this was a very emotional experience for me, as it is for many, and it was a grace-filled moment. In the months leading up to that retreat I had begun going down the wrong path. I had started partying and drinking. With my conversion, the direction of my life changed, and it changed permanently. Ever since then I have striven, with lesser or greater success, to be a disciple of Jesus Christ.

One thing my conversion didn't change, however, was who I was: a sixteen-year-old kid. I was immature, judgmental, arrogant, and prideful. As such, I still did stupid stuff. I knew these things weren't in keeping with being Christ's disciple, and I would usually regret them afterward. So I would go into my bedroom, kneel at my bed, tell Jesus I was sorry, and ask him to forgive me. And guess what happened? Nothing, at least as far as I could tell. I would return to doing stupid stuff, which would lead me back to asking for forgiveness. Lather, rinse, repeat.

I became frustrated, not to mention worried. Maybe God wasn't listening to me. Maybe I wasn't asking the right way, and so God *didn't* forgive me. Maybe that's why I didn't see any improvement in the way I acted. This was a real issue in my spiritual life at that time.

Fast-forward to my senior year in college. I was preparing to be received into the Catholic Church at Easter. Since, as a Protestant, I had already been baptized as an infant, and obviously committed many sins thereafter, I needed to go to confession before receiving Communion at the Easter Vigil. I spent quite a while in that confessional, but the priest was patient and compassionate and made sure I made a good confession. Then we came to the part I was waiting for:

God, the Father of mercies, through the death and the resurrection of his Son has reconciled the world to himself and sent the Holy Spirit among us for the forgiveness of sins; through the ministry of the Church may God give you pardon and peace, and *I absolve you from your sins* in the name of the Father, and of the Son, and of the Holy Spirit.

Those words—"I absolve you of your sins"—had a dramatic impact on me. I didn't have to guess whether God forgave me. I didn't have to wonder whether I had asked for forgiveness properly. I knew—with moral certainty—that I was forgiven, because I heard it said explicitly. A great burden had been lifted, and I walked out of that confessional a new man. (It helped that every Catholic member of my pro-life group, who'd been waiting in line behind me, gave me a rousing round of applause when I came out.) Even though I sinned many times after that confession, I now knew the remedy for those inevitable falls: sacramental confession.

I Am a Man of Unclean Lips

My nascent desire for forgiveness in high school was a natural reaction to coming into the presence of God during that altar call. When the prophet Isaiah is taken up into a vision of heaven, he sees the Lord enthroned and hears the seraphim crying out, "Holy, holy, holy is the Lord of hosts; the whole earth is full of his glory" (Isa. 6:3). His first reaction is to recognize his own unworthiness: "And I said: 'Woe is me! For I am lost; for I am a man of unclean lips, and I dwell in the midst of a people of unclean lips; for my eyes have seen the King, the Lord of hosts!'" (Isa. 6:5). The prophet recognizes the great gulf between himself and the all-holy One, and he immediately confesses his unworthiness. In response, the Lord allows Isaiah into his presence:

> Then flew one of the seraphim to me, having in his hand a burning coal which he had taken with tongs from the altar. And he touched my mouth, and said: "Behold, this has touched your lips; your guilt is taken away, and your sin forgiven." And I heard the voice of the Lord saying,

"Whom shall I send, and who will go for us?" Then I said, "Here am I! Send me" (Isa. 6:6–8).

It's not just in the Old Testament that we see such a reaction. St. Peter responds in a similar way when he first realizes who Jesus is. By all accounts, Peter is a simple man. He's a fisherman, and his concerns are primarily practical: Is the boat ready? What kind of weather will we have tonight? Am I in the right location to drop the nets?

But Peter is also a man of great faith. When Jesus tells him, "Put out into the deep and let down your nets for a catch," he answers, "Master, we toiled all night and took nothing! But at your word I will let down the nets" (Luke 5:4–5). As we know, Peter and his companions make a great catch of fish, such that their nets break and their boats start to sink. For others in this situation, the reaction might be shock, or gratitude, or awe. But Peter's is a deep sense of unworthiness: "Depart from me, for I am a sinful man, O Lord" (Luke 5:8).

What does Peter's sinfulness have to do with this catch of fish? As an experienced fisherman, Peter understands that Christ worked a miracle: there is no way he just made a "lucky guess" about where to find a lot of fish (he was a carpenter, not a fisherman, after all). So Peter realizes he's in the presence of the All-Holy, which illuminates his soul like a floodlight. Now, if a person has been wallowing in the mud in a dark room, he might not realize how dirty he is. If a small light comes on, his filth might be more apparent, but not to its full extent. But if a bright light shines in the room, then he will discover exactly how dirty he is. That's what Peter experienced: in the presence of divine light, he realized he was mired in sin. Other great saints throughout history likewise lament that they are the greatest of sinners, which might sound over scrupulous or hyperbolic to us, but that's because we're comparing them with ordinary sinners like ourselves. But the saints are comparing themselves with the all-holy Lord who has no sin in him. We see the saints in only a dim light, but they see themselves under the divine light of Christ.

The Catholic Evangelist's "Secret Weapon"

What is the ultimate goal of evangelization? Conversion, of course. We desire that someone change the direction of his life by becoming Catholic (or returning to the Church) and following Christ faithfully from then on. But, more practically, what is the initial goal of the Catholic evangelist? What first step do we want someone to take? Attend Mass? Go to the church picnic? Say a specific prayer?

When I was a Protestant evangelist, my goal was to get people to pray the "sinner's prayer." One example of this prayer is the following:

> Father, I know that I have broken your laws and my sins have separated me from you. I am truly sorry, and now I want to turn away from my past sinful life toward you. Please forgive me, and help me avoid sinning again. I believe that your son, Jesus Christ, died for my sins, was resurrected from the dead, is alive, and hears my prayer. I invite Jesus to become the Lord of my life, to rule and reign in my heart from this day forward. Please send your Holy Spirit to help me obey you and to do your will for the rest of my life. In Jesus' name I pray. Amen.

Promoting the "sinner's prayer" made evangelizing simple: if I got someone to pray it, I had myself a convert and I could move on to someone else. Once I became Catholic, however, I realized that there was much more to conversion than simply saying a prayer like this.

So, where should the Catholic evangelist direct potential converts? Straight to the confessional. For all but the non-baptized, sacramental confession is the doorway to (or back to) the Church. In the United States, non-practicing Catholics and baptized Protestants number over 200 million people. And for every one of them, confession is necessary to start or restart a relationship with Jesus Christ in the Catholic Church.

One of the key insights of the New Evangelization is that we are facing something unprecedented in Church history: millions of baptized Catholics who are no longer "practicing" Catholics, even if some go to Mass on occasion, such as on Christmas and Easter.

Let's define "practicing Catholic." Many people think of the term as describing someone who goes to Mass each Sunday. But in truth the term should be defined more restrictively, in accordance with the precepts of the Church. A practicing Catholic goes to Mass each Sunday, *and also* goes to confession at least once a year. By this standard, surveys have shown, fewer than 10 percent of Catholics in the United States are "practicing." That makes *lapsed Catholics* the largest "religious body" in America!

They represent the "low-hanging fruit" for Catholic evangelists. Why? First, they are already attached to the Church in three ways: sacramentally (they've been baptized), socially (they usually self-identify as Catholic even if they haven't darkened a church door in ages), and genealogically (most have Catholic parents). So when we talk about Catholicism to them, they don't find it an alien religion, even if they have many misconceptions about it. Second, they are ripe for evangelization because they have an easy entry back into the Church: confession (though some might need an annulment first).

Confession is also a necessary step for baptized Protestants. Of course, converting to Catholicism is usually a long process for a Protestant, often taking years. He has to grapple with Catholic doctrines such as purgatory and transubstantiation, overcome prejudices, and risk losing friends. But before he can receive confirmation and the Eucharist to become a full member of the Church, he must go to confession. This step is a natural one, however, as usually the convert sees his old life in an entirely new way and understands that he must be reconciled to Christ before being united to him through his Church.

Confession, then, *must* be the focus of our evangelization efforts—it must be what we direct souls to, and it must be integral to our proclamation of the gospel.

We Cannot Share What We Do Not Have

The Catholic evangelist shouldn't just promote confession—he should *go* to confession. The greatest evangelists in Church history were also saints, and this isn't a coincidence. They could speak of the power of God's forgiveness because they had experienced it themselves. Anyone serious about Catholic evangelization should go to confession regularly—at least once a month—for three reasons:

We want to be saints

The best salesmen are those who believe in their product. If we love our Catholic faith and want to share it with others, then we should strive to be the best Catholics we can, meaning *saints*. As the French Catholic writer Leon Bloy put it, "The only real sadness, the only real failure, the only great tragedy in life, is not to become a saint."

We want to witness to God's forgiveness

St. Paul is the greatest evangelist the Church has ever produced. Essential to his method was to tell the story of his former life as a persecutor of Christ. If God could forgive even me, he preached, you can be assured that he will forgive you. By receiving God's forgiveness in our own lives, we can witness to that forgiveness to others. Our broken world desperately needs this.

We don't want to be hypocritical

If we're asking people to change their lives radically in conformity with Christ's, why will they listen to us if we aren't attempting to do the same? None of us is perfect, and our message will resound more loudly if we acknowledge our own sinfulness and need for God's forgiveness. No one likes a politician who says one thing and does another in his private life; likewise, no one will respect an evangelist who preaches Christ to others, but doesn't live Christ in his or her own life. Nothing kills a witness faster than that.

If You Promote It, They Will Come

A popular program in many dioceses is called *The Light Is On*. Pioneered by the Archdiocese of Washington, it promotes going to confession during Lent. To do that, typically a diocese will offer confession at the same time in every parish, either weekly or on one specific day. So every parish might offer confession, say, on every Wednesday evening of Lent at 7 p.m.

I initiated *The Light Is On* the first Lent I was working at the diocesan level in evangelization. We produced TV commercials, bus ads, radio spots, and billboards promoting confession. And, of course, all the parishes advertised the added confession times in their bulletins. After Lent I talked to a number of priests to see if the program was a success. What I heard astounded me—people who had been away for twenty, thirty, even forty years had returned to confession simply because they had been asked! One priest in a tiny parish off the beaten track reported that every week of the program he had at least one penitent who hadn't been to confession in twenty or more years.

But in general, confession has been neglected by Catholics, and for self-fulfilling reasons: it isn't promoted because no one goes to it, and no one goes to it because it isn't promoted. And in many—perhaps most—parishes it's only available at limited times, such as on Saturdays from 4:15 to 4:45 p.m. And usually the lines aren't very long, appearing to justify the limited availability. Once I was giving a talk on confession and someone said to me afterward, "That's all well and good, but no one actually goes to confession anymore." But confession is exactly what our world needs today, and if we promote it better, I'm convinced we'll see results.

I once attended a parish that had the usual Saturday afternoon half hour of confession. But when a new pastor was assigned, he immediately announced a change in the confession schedule: confessions would now be heard half an hour before each daily Mass and an hour on Saturday mornings, as well as the old Saturday afternoon time. He also preached about the importance of confession at the next few Sunday Masses. The result? Even though confession was now far more available than before, the lines were longer. Once parishioners were encouraged to go to confession, they went. Sometimes, it's as simple as that.

Catholic evangelization, in essence, seeks to bring others into an encounter with Christ. For those who have been baptized, confession is the place for this encounter. It's the re-establishment of that "personal relationship" that every disciple of Christ should have. Confession changes the trajectory of a person's life. No longer is that life self-centered; now it is Christ-centered. Because of this, *the single most effective activity of any Catholic evangelist is to promote the sacrament of confession.*

Example

St. John Vianney, the Curé of Ars

St. John Vianney was born to a devout Catholic family in late-eighteenth-century France, when Catholics were being persecuted, and many martyred, under the French Revolution and its Reign of Terror. At Vianney's First Communion, the windows of the church were covered so the candles could not be seen from outside. Profoundly impressed by the courage of the priests he knew as a boy, he desired to emulate them and was ordained a priest himself at the age of twenty-nine.

After the Revolution, it eventually became safe again to practice the Faith openly, but by then many Frenchmen were ignorant of or indifferent to it. Vianney determined to re-evangelize his fellow Catholics and help them return to the Church. He was assigned as the parish priest in Ars, a town with only 230 residents, most of them former Catholics. But he engaged them all and exhorted them to rediscover their faith and abandon their immoral ways. He himself performed great penances, led Eucharistic adoration, and prayed without ceasing for his flock.

But more than anything, Vianney promoted the sacrament of confession. He sat in the confessional for ten or more hours a day, sometimes as many as eighteen. At first, he sat there almost alone, with few penitents. But over time his saintly demeanor and perseverance drew more and more people to confession. Word spread throughout the country of this holy and humble priest and his devotion to the sacrament. By the time he was in his forties, people traveled from great distances to confess to him. Eventually, the lines for his confessional were so long that people had to wait long hours, even days to see him. It is believed that he heard up to twenty thousand confessions each year.

Examination

- Do I promote the sacrament of confession in all my evangelistic activities?

- Do I practice what I preach and regularly go to confession?

Exploration

- Why do you think confession is so neglected today?

- Why did Peter think first of his sinfulness after the miraculous catch of fish?

- When was the last time you invited someone to go to confession?

Exercise

- Make it a regular practice to go to confession at least once a month.

- Volunteer at your parish to promote confession. Ask your pastor how you can help make confession more widely practiced.

- Order or download the Catholic Answers tract on confession. Give it to a Protestant friend who is curious but skeptical about the sacrament.

11

Jesus Arouses Our Reverence

When my parents were young, people dressed nicely to travel by plane or go to a ballgame. Adults, unless they were close friends, addressed one another as Mr. Hoffman and Mrs. Martin, not Alex and Jenny. But now we live in a casual culture, and that kind of formality seems alien.

Casualness has crept into our practice of religion too. Many Protestant churches are actually *trying* to become more casual—coffee shops connected to the sanctuary, relaxed dress codes, and an informal way of relating to Jesus, who is looked on more as our best friend than as our Lord.

Catholics, too, are embracing this trend toward casualness, even though Church tradition has always been one of reverence in our worship, which implies a certain formality. The purpose of this reverence is to glorify God, and when it is absent it impairs our evangelization efforts. After all, if you treat your own faith casually, why should anyone else take it seriously? Reverence, then, is an essential element of our faith, and also essential to the success of a Catholic evangelist.

Encounter

The appearance to John on the island of Patmos (Rev. 1:9–20)

⁹I John, your brother, who share with you in Jesus the tribulation and the kingdom and the patient endurance, was on the island called Patmos on account of the word

of God and the testimony of Jesus. [10]I was in the Spirit on the Lord's day, and I heard behind me a loud voice like a trumpet [11]saying, "Write what you see in a book and send it to the seven churches, to Ephesus and to Smyrna and to Pergamum and to Thyatira and to Sardis and to Philadelphia and to Laodicea."

[12]Then I turned to see the voice that was speaking to me, and on turning I saw seven golden lampstands, [13]and in the midst of the lampstands one like a son of man, clothed with a long robe and with a golden girdle round his breast; [14]his head and his hair were white as white wool, white as snow; his eyes were like a flame of fire, [15]his feet were like burnished bronze, refined as in a furnace, and his voice was like the sound of many waters; [16]in his right hand he held seven stars, from his mouth issued a sharp two-edged sword, and his face was like the sun shining in full strength.

[17]When I saw him, I fell at his feet as though dead. But he laid his right hand upon me, saying, "Fear not, I am the first and the last, [18]and the living one; I died, and behold I am alive for evermore, and I have the keys of Death and Hades. [19]Now write what you see, what is and what is to take place hereafter. [20]As for the mystery of the seven stars which you saw in my right hand, and the seven golden lampstands, the seven stars are the angels of the seven churches and the seven lampstands are the seven churches.

Taking Jesus to the Streets

Most Catholics are familiar with Eucharistic processions, in which the sacred host is placed in a monstrance and held aloft by a member of the clergy as he leads the faithful around the church or its parking lot, or through neighboring streets. Catholics have been conducting Eucharistic processions for hundreds of years, and it is one of my own favorite practices—and a great way to literally bring Jesus to the streets.

I once participated in a Eucharistic procession at a public university that was near a beach and known for its laid-back atmosphere. As at most public universities today, the students were almost uniformly irreligious. Not necessarily *anti*-religious: they just saw no reason to let religion intrude on their beach lifestyle. The small Catholic group on campus decided to hold a Eucharistic procession through the middle of the main campus square. I heard about it and decided to bring my family.

Unfortunately, attendance was light—around two dozen of us in total. But the priest who led us was enthusiastic about the Faith and gave us courage. From a secular perspective, the procession must have seemed like aliens landing on campus: here was a fully vested priest holding up a golden object, with a couple of dozen people following him singing religious hymns. Most of the students had probably never seen anything like it. Remembering their expressions as we passed by, I'm actually sure they hadn't. Everyone stopped what they were doing—going to class, snacking or studying on the grass, conversing—to watch us. Some looked bewildered; others smirked. But they all noticed us.

Afterward, one student approached us and asked what it was all about: "What religion are you?" When we told her we were Catholic, she nodded and said, "That's great, that's great." She was impressed that we believed in something so deeply that we would treat it with such respect and reverence. Some other students expressed similar sentiments. This gave us the opportunity to explain our faith. So you see, reverence can be an important component of evangelization.

Falling at His Feet

Each chapter of this book centers on an encounter that Jesus had with someone before his Ascension into heaven—except this chapter, which focuses on one of the only two encounters the Bible records as taking place *after* his Ascension: the encounter with St. John the Apostle described at the beginning of the book of Revelation (the other encounter was with Paul on the road to Damascus). Like everything in Revelation, it is full of mystery, but it teaches us an important lesson about reverence.

First some backstory. It was John the Apostle himself, the disciple "whom Jesus loved" (John 13:23), who wrote the book of Revelation. It was he who leaned on the Lord's breast at the Last Supper; he who alone among the apostles was at the foot of the Cross; and he to whom Jesus entrusted the care of his mother. If anyone could ever claim to be Jesus' best friend, it was John the Apostle.

After the Ascension, John faithfully spread the gospel far and wide. Near the end of his life, he was exiled to the island of Patmos "on account of the word of God and the testimony of Jesus" (Rev. 1:9). While on Patmos he had a vision, in which the first thing he saw was Jesus. Try to imagine your own reaction had you been John. The man you've devoted your whole life to, the man you love above all others, is now standing before you. Do you run to embrace him? Do you tell him all you've done for him since you last saw him? Do you weep in gratitude? All these would be natural reactions for someone who has just been reunited with his best friend after many years' separation.

But none of these were John's reaction: "When I saw him, I fell at his feet as though dead" (Rev. 1:17). For he sees Jesus not merely as the former teacher to whom he was devoted as a student, but as the Lord of the universe, worthy of worship, adoration, and praise. In other words, John's reaction is "the fear of the Lord" so often mentioned in the Old Testament. All the symbols John uses to describe Jesus—head and hair as white as snow, eyes of fire, a two-edged sword coming from his mouth—seek to express the great glory of the Lord.

Some of us might think, "Well, if I saw Jesus reappear today I would fall down too!" Yet we *do* see Jesus reappear today—during Mass at the consecration of the Eucharist. Do we fall down in worship and adoration? Do we treat this as an encounter with the Lord of the universe?

There is a popular story, probably apocryphal, about a Muslim who attends Mass. He has a basic understanding of Catholicism, so he knows what we believe about the Real Presence. After Mass he tells his Catholic friend, "If I believed what you Catholics believe about Communion—that it is really God you are receiving—I would fall to my knees and crawl up the Communion line."

Now, the Islamic conception of God is very different from the Catholic conception; Muslims see God primarily as a master, while we see him primarily as a father. So of course there will be a difference in how we approach God. But the point of the story is a valid one: do we treat our relationship with Christ—whose most intimate point of contact is in Communion—with reverence? Do we, like John the Apostle, fall down (in our case, figuratively) in adoration and worship when we encounter him? Or do we think of him as merely a friend who helps us in times of trouble?

Mass Evangelization

Our attitude toward Jesus, and our worship of him, affects how we think of the Mass and its relationship to evangelization. For an Evangelical Protestant, there is no better way

to evangelize than to invite a friend to a church service. After all, many of their services include an "altar call," which
asks non-Christians or fallen-away Christians to come forward and give their lives to Jesus. Overall, many of these
services are geared toward potential converts (Protestants
call it being "seeker-friendly"). On the other hand, for the
non-Catholic visitor the Mass can be a confusing mix of
standing, kneeling, sitting, singing, and listening. As a Protestant I went to Mass many times before I even had the
slightest idea what was going on. Because of this difficulty
some Catholics advocate simplifying the Mass so that, like
Protestant services, it can attract more converts.

But the Mass is not primarily a tool of evangelization.
Let's look back to the days of the first Christians, who lived
in the Roman Empire as a small, often persecuted sect. At
that time attendance at Mass was restricted to those who
had already been baptized. Granted, the danger of being
Catholic had something to do with this rule. At any time
a persecution might flare up, and if it did, you didn't want
your enemies witnessing your participation in an outlawed
religious ceremony. But this was not the only reason for re-
stricting attendance. The sacraments of the Church were
called "the mysteries," and celebrating them was considered
the most worshipful act one could engage in. To allow the
non-baptized even to witness this would seem in some way
a sacrilege. Even after Christianity was legalized, the non-
baptized were required to leave the Church after the first
part of Mass (what we call the "Liturgy of the Word") out of
respect for the Eucharist. We see remnants of that practice in
the Eastern-rite liturgy's cry "The doors! The doors!" that
precedes the Eucharistic prayer: it is a call to the guardians
of the doors to ensure that the unbaptized do not witness the
Eucharistic sacrifice.

We can learn two lessons from the early Church practice: (1) the celebration of Mass itself was not considered a tool for attracting people to the Christian Faith—since non-Christians weren't even allowed to attend Mass, it could not be used to evangelize them; and (2) this apparent restriction did not negatively impact the early Church's evangelization efforts, which were enormously successful. Christians succeeded in attracting others to the Faith not by bringing them to an attractive liturgy, but by living and preaching the power of the gospel. Over the centuries the Church added much pageantry to its liturgies, *but the focus of those additions was always to give greater glory to God, not to attract converts.*

Many Catholics today are frustrated by the seeming complexity and strangeness of the Mass. They want to make it "relevant," more like entertainment, in order to attract more people. But this is a project doomed to failure. Witness the cringe-worthy efforts by aging baby boomers to copy the latest cultural fad in their desire to "reach out" to estranged Catholics: sad stabs at "hip" music, priests turning Mass into Comedy Central, and even lightshows more appropriate to Chuck E. Cheese's than St. Charles Catholic Church. Meanwhile, the most creative minds in the world spend billions each year producing entertainment for the masses. If the choice is between Hollywood's polished product and the poor imitation found at the local Catholic parish, most will choose the real thing.

Does that mean the Mass can't attract potential converts? Of course it can. But the secret isn't trying to beat the culture at its own game. Rather, *let's play our game*— one at which we already excel. For two thousand years the Church has celebrated the most sublime—and attractive—liturgical celebrations known to man. Paradoxically, it is by putting the focus on God, not man, that people are attracted to the transcendent grandeur of a life of faith. A banal focus on pleasing people, on the other hand, leaves them unsatisfied and looking elsewhere to quench their thirst for the transcendent.

Traditionally, the chief ends of the Mass are said to be fourfold: adoration, atonement, thanksgiving, and petition. "Evangelization" is not included. This doesn't mean that the Mass has no relationship to evangelization; after all, the Mass is the source and summit of the Christian faith, so it relates to *everything* in Christian life. But although evangelization is not a primary *purpose* of the Mass, it is one of its *fruits*. Assisting at the Mass, sacramentally uniting ourselves to the sacrifice of Calvary, each Catholic receives the strength to go out and make disciples of all nations.

By confusing fruit with purpose, many Catholics denigrate, unwittingly or not, the celebration of the holy sacrifice of the Mass. Efforts to make it "relevant" in the end make it a barrier to true evangelization. By focusing on the horizontal (directed toward man) rather than on the vertical (directed toward God), our priorities become inverted, and the result neither gives glory to God nor attracts those who are lost. By aspiring first and foremost to give glory to the Almighty, however, we also receive what is needed to bring people to him. As our Lord said, "Seek first his kingdom and his righteousness, and all these things shall be yours as well" (Matt. 6:33).

Making Reverence Practical

We might ask, "What does this have to do with my everyday practice of evangelization?"

Reverence is essential to the witness we give, and it can have a decisive impact on evangelization. Imagine a state dinner with the president of the United States. Everyone is formally dressed, the best presidential china is laid out, and the band strikes up "Hail to the Chief" as the president enters the room. What would you think of someone who walked in a side door, talking on a cell phone and wearing cutoff jeans and a heavy-metal T-shirt? (I'm pretty sure I know what the Secret Service would think.) You would assume that this person had little respect for the office of the presidency, and perhaps for the United States itself. If he were to tell a foreign visitor how great the American form of government is, don't you think his slovenly appearance and casual behavior would in some way lessen the impact of his words?

Likewise, the impact of our Catholic evangelization is lessened if we ignore reverence. If we are casual in the practice of our faith, that signals that it's not very important to us. So why should anyone take us seriously about it?

Now admittedly, unless you're a bishop, a priest, or a member of your parish's liturgy committee, most of us don't have any influence over how Mass is celebrated. But we can show reverence in our own lives. One way is by treating the Lord's Day reverently. As the *Catechism* states:

> On Sundays and other holy days of obligation, the faithful are to refrain from engaging in work or activities that hinder the worship owed to God, the joy proper to the Lord's Day, the performance of the works of mercy, and the appropriate relaxation of mind and body. Family needs or important social service can legitimately excuse from the obligation of Sunday rest. The faithful should see to it that legitimate excuses do not lead to habits prejudicial to religion, family life, and health (CCC 2185).

Yet in today's culture many things have intruded on Sundays, hindering our ability to treat it as the Lord's Day. Youth sports are one example: many leagues now schedule games and tournaments on Sundays, even in the morning hours, when most Christians are in church. A few years ago my son was on a baseball team in an important all-star tournament. We had avoided putting him on a team that played games on Sundays, but in this case, due to some weather cancellations, the championship game was scheduled for Sunday morning. The coach texted the parents the night before to let us know, and I hesitated. This was a very important game, but I didn't want my son playing on a Sunday morning. As I deliberated, another parent—whose son was one of the team's stars—texted back that her son couldn't make it; their family would be going to church instead (they were Evangelicals). I was ashamed that I hesitated while this other family was clear about their priorities. I followed up with a text stating that my son wouldn't be there either.

In the end, the game was rescheduled and we were able to play (our coach, I hear, made a convincing plea to the league about the injustice of penalizing a team for having players who were religious). During the game I approached the parent who had said her son couldn't make it, and told her I appreciated her witness. She had six children, and all played sports. But she and her husband had realized long ago, she said, that sports could dominate their family life and interfere with going to church. They decided not to let that happen, so they had a strict policy of no games on Sunday mornings, no matter what. This witness had a powerful impact on me and on everyone involved with the team: we saw that they took their faith seriously and had reverence for the Lord's Day. How many Catholic families can say the same?

Seek First the Kingdom of God

Here's an important point about that family's actions: they didn't skip the game in order to evangelize anyone. They did it out of respect for God and the Lord's Day. Yet it bore fruit in positively witnessing their faith to others.

Sometimes we make evangelization an idol—our highest priority is to attract others to the Faith! Since we live in a casual culture, we believe making our faith casual will attract those in our culture. But our faith is countercultural, and as such it will always attract sincere seekers. Consider the attendance at a typical Latin Mass: it isn't mostly nostalgic older folks, but rather young families who value reverence. Their attendance is a great witness, for when other people see them being serious about their faith, they become curious as to the source of the attraction.

We must always keep in mind that being Catholic is not like being a member of a social club or political movement. We practice the Faith to glorify God, which we were created to do. When we practice our faith as casually as we would attend a football game or go to the beach, we say with our actions that God isn't much more important than the quarterback of our favorite team or catching a wicked wave. The casualness of our culture doesn't satisfy that longing of the human heart to transcend this world and be united with He Who Is.

God is unlike everything around us, and our actions should speak this truth.

Perhaps the most famous story of reverence leading to evangelization involves the conversion of Russia. Near the end of the first millennium, Vladimir, the pagan leader of Russia, wanted to unite his country. He reckoned that a single religion could help him achieve that goal. He sent forth emissaries to examine the major religions of his time: Christianity (both in Rome and in Constantinople), Judaism, and Islam. Vladimir didn't like the dietary restrictions of either Judaism or Islam, and although he found no objections to Christianity as practiced in Rome, he also wasn't attracted to its (at that time) simple liturgy. But when his emissaries returned from attending a divine liturgy in Constantinople, they exclaimed, "We knew not whether we were in heaven or on earth, for surely there is no such splendor or beauty anywhere upon earth. We cannot describe it to you. Only we know that God dwells there among men, and that their service surpasses the worship of all other places. We cannot forget that beauty." The reverence of that liturgy—with its singing, incense, colorful vestments, and beautiful surrounding architecture—led Vladimir, and Russia with him, to convert to Eastern Christianity. So although the worshipers in Constantinople that day were celebrating their liturgy to glorify God, one of its fruits was the conversion of an entire country!

We too need to be reverent, not in order to evangelize but because God deserves it. But a fruit of that reverence will be that others will see how seriously we take our faith, which can lead them to consider it for themselves. In an age with so many people mired in the darkness of apathy toward religion and even life itself, our reverence is a bright light drawing others into communion with our Lord.

Example

St. Eric of Sweden

Eric of Sweden was crowned king of his country in the year 1150. During his reign he established Catholicism as Sweden's religion and built the first large church ever erected there. After his victory over pagan armies, he sent St. Henry, bishop of Uppsala, out to evangelize his people.

Eric's zeal for the Faith was not popular with many Swedish nobles, who wanted to maintain the status quo, as is typical of men in power. And the status quo for centuries had been paganism, which Eric's reign threatened to eliminate. After some years, a group of these nobles made an alliance with Magnus, the son of the king of Denmark. They formed a large army that included both Danes and rebel Swedes. On the Feast of the Ascension, this army marched off to overthrow Eric.

That day, King Eric was hearing Mass when his aides told him that the rebel army was closing in on his position. He answered calmly, "Let us at least finish the sacrifice; the rest of the feast I shall keep elsewhere." For Eric, nothing—not even his own safety—was more important than worshipping our Lord in the Mass.

After Mass ended, he recommended his soul to God and went out to meet the opposing force. His opponents rushed him, knocked him from his horse, and cut off his head. It was May 18, 1161. His witness to the Faith—including his reverence for the Mass—helped to evangelize his land and make Sweden a Catholic nation.

Examination

- Do I treat God with the reverence due to him?

- Do I ever show irreverence toward the Faith in an attempt to make it more relatable to others?

Exploration

- What does reverence toward something say about how one values it?

- How does the story of Jesus driving out the money-changers (John 2:13–25) illustrate the importance of reverence?

- Read 1 Corinthians 11. How does St. Paul show reverence for the Eucharist?

Exercise

- Next Sunday set aside time (apart from Mass) for prayer and meditation.

- Next time you attend Mass, consider whether your clothes reflect proper reverence for the Lord.

- Read *The Spirit of the Liturgy* by Romano Guardini (it can be downloaded online).

Jesus, Model Evangelist

Years ago a popular trend among Christians was to ask "What would Jesus do?" It seemed you couldn't walk into a Protestant church without seeing "WWJD?" on bracelets, T-shirts, and banners. The idea behind the catch phrase, of course, was to encourage Christians to model their lives completely after the Lord. And this indeed is how all Christians should live: conforming their lives so much to Christ's that they can say with St. Paul, "it is no longer I who live, but Christ who lives in me" (Gal. 2:20). No matter the time or culture we live in, we must look to Jesus as the model for everything we do in life, including evangelization.

Jesus was the perfect evangelizer: he thirsted for the salvation of souls, to the point of giving up his life for them. He confronted the devil directly, worked tirelessly for the conversion of souls, had no tolerance for sin, and demanded that his followers fully embrace the entirety of his message. What were the results? At the time of his death he had perhaps two dozen followers, and even fewer were present at his Crucifixion. Compared with other religious leaders, such as Muhammad, Jesus seemed to have failed in his mission. Yet history proves that the methods of evangelization he modeled were astoundingly successful, for soon after his death his followers began to convert the known world. Within a few generations Christians could be found in every city and town in the Roman Empire, and beyond.

We too have been called to convert the world. Like Jesus, we may never travel much beyond our birthplace, and may never interact deeply with more than a few hundred people. Yet if we model ourselves on Jesus, we can have a life-changing impact on those around us.

You have a circle of influence—your family, your friends, your neighbors, your coworkers, even the people you bump into regularly at the grocery store. You can use this influence to direct people toward Christ and his Church, or you can use it to direct people away from them. If you follow the example of Jesus and the principles of the great Catholic evangelizers of the past, as outlined in this book, you can have as profound an influence as Christ's first followers, who transformed a pagan culture into a Christian one and saw countless souls turn away from the path of destruction to the path of eternal life in Jesus Christ.

Now let's get started!

Eric Sammons

A former Evangelical, Eric Sammons entered the Catholic Church in 1993. He has been involved in Catholic evangelization efforts for more than two decades, including five years as a diocesan director of evangelization. He is the father of seven children, author of several books, and a professional writer/editor. His website "Swimming Upstream" can be found at ericsammons.com.